MW01155335

TABLE OF CONTENTS

Spanish Grammar for Intermediate Learners

Learn and Improve Easily with this Complete Spanish Workbook for Adults

Textbook and Workbook

Isabel Navarro Torres – Dani Rangel Nieto – Julie Helliwell

INTRODUCTION

¿Estás listo? Are you ready to get started on a brand-new chapter in your journey to learning Spanish? First of all, we'd like to reassure you that you're making the right decision. If you're reading these lines, you've picked this book with the intention of working on your Spanish skills. However, you couldn't have picked this book at random, because this isn't just any manual for people interested in learning a little bit of Spanish. No, by opening these pages, you've ventured into a very special level of learning that isn't immediately open to all beginners; this is an Intermediate book.

Just like this book, you are a very special student. Reaching the Intermediate level is a fantastic achievement. Firstly, it shows that you are genuinely committed to learning a new language. This means that your chances of becoming completely and confidently fluent in Spanish are higher than ever before, and most definitely better than the rest of the population just getting started in their studies. It's time to make the most of this opportunity and dive headfirst into this new chapter.

Before starting this book, with all certainty, you've had some contact with the Spanish language. Have you enjoyed dancing and singing along to the soulful and passionate songs? Perhaps you've picked up one of those classic and awe-inspiring books in Spanish you long to read. It's likely that you've started noticing and clinging to the bits and pieces of Spanish dialogue you hear in the street, in movies, or on television. But it's so much more than that, isn't it? You've put in the work, you've studied the basics, and you should be proud of the knowledge you have collected. The best tool you will find in your journey as a beginner is our book *Spanish Grammar Guide For Beginners - The Extensive And Easy Step-By-Step Approach To Learning Spanish Grammar*. Well, it's time to take the next step.

After successfully completing our guide for beginners, you will have a satisfying grasp of the foundations of the Spanish language. We are talking about sentence method and structure, the subjects and their pronouns, and the most commonly used verbs, adjectives, and tenses. But this also included an additional array of wonderful new information. You've learned about the numbers, colors, days and months, family members, parts of the body, food, and weather. These colorful and diverse pieces of knowledge can offer you the opportunity of forming simple sentences and maintain basic conversations successfully. So, you may ask yourself, what comes next?

What you have in your hands right now is a very practical, thorough, and methodically-created guide. In this book, you will find step-by-step lessons that have taken into account everything a student needs to master the Intermediate level in Spanish. The description of every subject is precise and written with students with your level of knowledge in mind. You'll notice the examples getting longer and more interesting, and you might find yourself feeling challenged. *Good*, this is how it's supposed to be; this is what learning feels like!

In this book, we present 25 uniquely written chapters, each focusing on an essential lesson in the process of learning Spanish. This level of learning will delve into more complex subjects that you are now capable of understanding. We will study the intricacies of adverbs, prepositions, and pronouns that will add a lot to the basic sentences you already know. The tenses and moods of Spanish will multiply in this book, resulting in a greater variety of sentences to enable you to communicate accurately and efficiently at this level.

Every chapter comes equipped with useful examples that will give you a glimpse into the everyday dialogue of native Spanish speakers. Then, a comprehensive and thorough explanation of the subject is followed by a series of carefully crafted exercises to help you fully assimilate the topic. You are also required to complete a group of translations to put this new knowledge to the test. Finally, you will find a short story included in every chapter. This small, creative piece is the perfect tool to practice your Spanish, stay sharp, and learn so much more than new words; you'll be learning about a whole new world.

This is the most exciting part, this is an exhilarating step, and all you need to do is keep in mind your goal every step of the way. Picture yourself speaking Spanish confidently, understanding a native speaker, and making your way through a Spanish-speaking city. Isn't that wonderful? Don't lose sight of your dreams, be ready to work hard and steadily, and the rewards will be more than worth it. So, go ahead, jump on the first chapter, learn the first lesson, and don't look back. *¡Buena suerte!*

Chapter 1
ADVERBS OF FREQUENCY

When learning how to speak a language like a native person, there are many little things that students need to know to become fluent. There are things about a language that will help new learners express themselves more naturally and effectively. One of these things is adverbs.

Adverbs are words that affect the verbs of a sentence. Adverbs add extra meaning to the verbs. The result is a sentence that's more complex and detailed. There are a few different types of adverbs, one of the most important and most commonly used ones are adverbs of frequency.

The use of adverbs of frequency will give more information about a sentence. These adverbs express how often or not an action is done. They let readers or listeners know the frequency with which a verb takes place. Usually, they are the answer to the question "¿Qué tan seguido?" (How often?). In Spanish, there are many adverbs of frequency.

Here you will learn the most common ones everyone needs to know.

- Siempre – Always

  o *Yo siempre me baño por la mañana.* – I always shower in the morning.

- Casi siempre – Almost always

  o *Ella casi siempre gana jugando al ajedrez.* – She almost always wins playing chess.

- Constantemente – Constantly

  o *Nosotros peleamos constantemente en casa.* - We fight constantly at home.

- Frecuentemente, con frecuencia – Frequently

  o *Tú viajas a Miami con frecuencia.* - You travel to Miami frequently.

- A menudo – Often

  - *Ellos van al cine a menudo.* - They go to the movie theater often.

- Mucho, muchas veces – Often, a lot, many times

  - *Usted trabaja mucho durante la semana.* - You work a lot during the week.

- Todos los días – Every day

  - *Nosotros hablamos todos los días en el colegio.* - We talk every day at school.

- Diariamente – Daily

  - *Samuel pasea su perro diariamente.* - Samuel walks his dog daily.

- Regularmente – Regularly

  - *Tú compras ropa nueva regularmente.* - You buy new clothes regularly.

- Normalmente - Usually

  - *Andreina normalmente come pizza los viernes.* - Andreina usually eats pizza on Fridays.

- Nunca – Never

  - *Ella nunca come carne.* - She never eats meat.

- Raramente – Rarely, Seldom

  - *Pablo raramente bebe alcohol.* – Pablo rarely drinks alcohol.

<u>Examples:</u>

1. Yo siempre tomo café por las mañanas.
   I always drink coffee in the morning.

2. Juan llega tarde a clase frecuentemente.
   Juan frequently arrives late to class.

3. Ella tiene que pasear al perro diariamente.
   She has to walk the dog daily.

Exercises:

1. Complete the sentences with the right adverb of frequency

   a. Yo me baño _____. (todos los días/a menudo)

   b. Carlos viaja en avión _____. (diariamente/frecuentemente)

   c. El sol _____ (normalmente/siempre) va a salir.

   d. Los perros se deben bañar _____. (diariamente/a menudo)

   e. La profesora da clases _____. (todos los días/frecuentemente)

   f. Después de la calma _____ (diariamente/siempre) viene la tormenta.

   g. En mi ciudad llueve _____. (todos los días / regularmente)

   h. En invierno cae nieve _____. (diariamente / casi siempre)

   i. El planeta Tierra gira _____. (a menudo / constantemente)

   j. Mi corazón late _____. (normalmente / constantemente)

2. Select the correct translation for each sentence

   a. Mi familia siempre viaja en verano

   b. La señora Cruz limpia la casa constantemente.

   c. Gerardo casi siempre se duerme viendo películas.

   d. Los ordenadores se actualizan regularmente.

   e. María toca el piano todos los días.

   f. Sara siempre llega tarde a las fiestas.

   g. Carol cambia de trabajo regularmente.

   h. Miguel compra ropa nueva constantemente.

   i. En mi casa siempre hay una gotera.

   j. En la noche normalmente hace frío.

   k. Gerardo almost always falls asleep during movies.

   l. Maria plays piano every day.

   m. Carol changes job regularly.

   n. My family always travels in summer.

   o. In my house there's always a leak.

   p. Sara always arrives late to parties.

   q. Miguel buys new clothes constantly.

   r. Mrs. Cruz cleans the house constantly.

   s. At night it's usually cold.

   t. Computers update regularly.

3. Highlight the adverb of frequency in the following sentences:

    a. Ashley visita a sus primos frecuentemente.

    b. Mi equipo favorito casi siempre gana.

    c. Ella llama a su madremadre todos los días.

    d. Nosotros caminamos juntos diariamente.

    e. Mi padrepadre lava su cochecoche frecuentemente.

    f. Mis primos se pelean constantemente.

    g. Él tiene que ver al doctor a menudo.

    h. Esa mujer se cae mucho.

    i. Pedro siempre gana jugando al ajedrez.

    j. Normalmente yo camino al trabajo.

4. Select the correct answer to the questions:

    a. ¿El sol sale por las mañanas?

        i. Siempre

        ii. A menudo

    b. ¿Duermes todas las noches?

        i. Muchas veces

        ii. Siempre

    c. ¿Los niños van al colegio?

        i. Normalmente

        ii. Casi todos los días

    d. ¿Olvidas las llaves de tu casa?

        i. Siempre

        ii. A menudo

    e. ¿Vas al cine?

        i. Casi siempre

        ii. Frecuentemente

    f. ¿El lunes es el primer día de la semana?

        i. Mucho

        ii. Siempre

    g. ¿Hace frío en la Antártida?

        i. Siempre

          ii. A menudo

   h. ¿Bebes agua?

          i. Todos los días

          ii. Mucho

   i. ¿El circo viene a la ciudad?

          i. Todos los días

          ii. A menudo

   j. ¿Tomas sopa en la comida?

          i. Regularmente

          ii. Siempre

5. Write full sentences using the words in each prompt:

   a. yo – pizza – frecuentemente – como

_____

   b. constantemente – respiramos – todos

_____

   c. pasear – ella – todos los días – le gusta

_____

   d. Valeria – temprano – casi siempre – duerme

_____

   e. ejercicio – Ricardo – hace – regularmente

_____

   f. estudia – mucho – Fabiana

_____

   g. padre – diariamente – tarde – trabaja

_____

   h. cocina – madre – pollo – muchas veces

_____

   i. odontólogo – frecuentemente – ir – recuerda

_____

   j. nuevas – a menudo – películas – estrenan

_____

Translations:

Translate the following sentences into English:

1. Yo siempre hago una gran fiesta por mi cumpleaños.

   _____

2. Mi padrepadre normalmente se viste de azul.

   _____

3. Los hermanos se pelean constantemente aunque se quieran.

   _____

4. El césped se debe cortar regularmente.

   _____

5. Es importante beber ocho vasos de agua todos los días.

   _____

6. Recuerda llamar a tus seres queridos a menudo.

   _____

7. Mi familia ha ido a la playa muchas veces.

   _____

8. Casi siempre que Paola viaja en avión, se marea.

   _____

9. Mi profesor hace exámenes sorpresa frecuentemente.

   _____

10. Víctor quiere dormir ocho horas diariamente.

_____

Story:

Las Nieves es un pequeño pero hermoso pueblo en las montañas. Allí viven solo unas cien personas, y todo funciona **perfectamente**. Los vecinos siempre se ayudan los unos a los otros. Las **calles** están constantemente limpias. Los **periódicos** tienen buenas noticias todos los días. Hay buenas **fiestas** regularmente a las que todos están invitados. Pero, a menudo, llega al pueblo una persona desconocida que puede cambiarlo todo.

Cerca de Las Nieves hay una gran ciudad, muy diferente al pequeño pueblo. Las personas que no encuentran **éxito** en la gran ciudad, constantemente se mudan al pueblo. Normalmente estas personas se adaptan a la vida **tranquila** de Las Nieves. Pero, muchas veces, estos desconocidos intentan aprovecharse de los vecinos del pueblo.

Por **ejemplo**, un año, llegó a Las Nieves un **mago**. Un hombre que fue **despedido** de un circo por casi siempre **arruinar** sus presentaciones. Este hombre intentó aprovecharse de sus nuevos vecinos en Las Nievas muchas veces. Pero este estafador se llevó una sorpresa al descubrir que el pequeño pueblo donde todo siempre salía bien estaba encantado… y él acababa de recibir una maldición por intentar estafarlos.

Vocabulary List:

1. perfectamente - perfectly
2. calles - streets
3. periódicos - newspapers
4. fiestas - parties
5. éxito - success
6. tranquila - quiet
7. ejemplo - example
8. mago - magician
9. despedido - fired
10. arruinar - ruining (to ruin)

Translated Story:

Las Nieves is a small but beautiful town in the mountains. Only about a hundred people live there, and everything works **perfectly**. Neighbors always help each other. The **streets** are constantly clean. The **newspapers** have good news every day. There are good **parties** regularly that everyone is invited to. But often, an unknown person comes to town who can change everything.

Near Las Nieves, there is a big city, very different from the small town. People who do not find **success** in the big city constantly move to the town. Usually, these people adapt to the **quiet** life of Las Nieves. But, many times, these strangers try to take advantage of the villagers.

For **example**, one year, a **magician** came to Las Nieves. A man who was **fired** from a circus for almost always **ruining** his performances. This man tried to take advantage of his new neighbors in Las Nieves many times. But this scammer was surprised to discover that the small town where everything always worked out was bewitched ... and he had just received a curse for trying to scam them.

Questions:

1. ¿Dónde se encuentra Las Nieves? _____

   Where is Las Nieves?

2. ¿Cuántas personas viven en Las Nieves? _____

   How many people live in Las Nieves?

3. ¿Cuál era la profesión del estafador? _____

   What was the profession of the scammer?

4. ¿Por qué ese hombre fue despedido? _____

   Why was that man fired?

5. ¿Qué estaba encantado? _____

   What was bewitched?

6. ¿Por qué el hombre fue maldecido? _____

   Why was the man cursed?

Answers:

1.

      a. Todos los días

      b. Frecuentemente

      c. Siempre

      d. A menudo

      e. Todos los días

      f. Siempre

      g. Regularmente

      h. Casi siempre

      i. Constantemente

      j. Constantemente

2.

      a-n

      b-r

      c-k

      d-t

      e-l

      f-p

      g-m

      h-q

      i-o

      j-s

3.

      a. Frecuentemente

      b. Casi siempre

      c. Todos los días

      d. Diariamente

      e. Frecuentemente

      f. Constantemente

g.   A menudo

h.   Mucho

i.   Siempre

j.   Normalmente

4.

    a. i

    b. ii

    c. ii

    d. ii

    e. ii

    f. ii

    g. i

    h. i

    i. ii

    j. i

5.

a. Yo como pizza frecuentemente.

b. Todos respiramos constantemente.

c. A ella le gusta pasear todos los días.

d. Valeria casi siempre se duerme temprano.

e. Ricardo hace ejercicio regularmente.

f. Fabiana estudia mucho.

g. Mi padrepadre trabaja hasta tarde diariamente.

h. Mi madremadre cocina pollo.

i. Recuerda ir frecuentemente al odontólogo.

j. A menudo estrenan películas nuevas.

Translations:

1. I always throw a big party on my birthday.
2. My dad usually dresses in blue.
3. Brothers fight constantly even if they love each other.
4. Grass must be cut regularly.
5. It's important to drink eight cups of water every day.
6. Remember to call your loved ones often.
7. My family has gone to the beach many times.
8. Almost always that Paola flies on a plane she gets dizzy.
9. My teacher makes surprise tests frequently.
10. Victor wants to sleep eight hours daily.

Story:

1. En las montañas.
2. Cien.
3. Mago.
4. Por arruinar sus presentaciones.
5. El pueblo.
6. Por intentar estafarlos.

Chapter 2
PREPOSITIONS

Prepositions are an important part of any language, and Spanish isn't an exception. They are a requirement to formulate fluent and cohesive sentences. Prepositions are essential parts of a sentence structure, just like nouns and verbs.

First, we have to understand what prepositions are. They are short words that indicate some kind of relation between two other words. The most common prepositions are used to describe location and time, plus things like ownership, origins, and causes.

In Spanish, there are many prepositions, and sometimes they might change their meaning depending on the context. It's one of those things that can't be simply memorized as a translation. It demands constant studying and practicing. Here we will guide you through the basics of understanding prepositions in Spanish.

Here is a list of the most used one-word prepositions in Spanish:

- De – of, about, from

    o *Esta clase es Español.* - This class is about Spanish.

- Desde – since, from

    o *Nosotros caminamos desde mi casa.* - We walked from my house.

- Hasta – as far as, up to, until

    o *Yo estudié hasta las diez.* - I studied until ten.

- A – at, to

    o *Ellas van a venir a mi casa.* - They are going to come to my house.

- Por – because of, for, by, through

    o *Tú estudias por esta razón.* - You study for this reason.

- En – in, into, by, inside, within, at

- *Jaime vive en Perú.* - Jaime lives in Peru.

- Ante – before, in the face of

  - *Yo no sé qué haré ante este problema.* - I don't know what I'll do in the face of this problem.

- Bajo – under, below

  - *Usted está bajo mucha presión.* - You are under a lot of pressure.

- Con – with

  - *Ella vive conmigo.* - She lives with me.

- Contra – against

  - *Nosotros jugamos contra ellos.* - We play against them.

- Durante – during

  - *Tú te dormiste durante la película.* - You fell asleep during the movie.

- Entre – between, among

  - *Nosotros estamos entre amigos.* - We are among friends.

- Hacia – toward, around

  - *Sara trabaja hacia una meta.* - Sara works toward a goal.

- Para – for, toward, to

  - *Yo estudio para aprender.* - I study to learn.

- Sobre – on, on top of, over, above, about

  - *Hay un libro sobre la mesa.* - There's a book on the table.

- Sin – without

  - *Yo no puedo vivir sin ella.* - I can't live without her.

<u>Examples:</u>

1. Este libro es *de* comida española.

   This book is *about* Spanish food.

2. Yo llevo viviendo aquí *desde* 2019.

   I have been living here *since* 2019.

3. Mi novia vive *en* Francia.

   My girlfriend lives *in* France.

4. Los perros sienten miedo *durante* una tormenta.

   Dogs feel afraid *during* a storm.

5. Este es un regalo *para* mi abuelo.

   This gift is *for* my grandfather.

Additionally, in Spanish, there are more complex alternatives, known as compound prepositions. These are prepositions that contain more than one word to express their meaning.

Here are a few of the most used ones.

- Además de – as well as, besides

    a. *Somos pareja además de colegas.* - We are partners as well as colleagues.

- Junto a – next to

    a. *Yo vivo junto a mi tía.* - I live next to my aunt.

- Al lado de – beside, to the side of

    a. *Hay una ventana al lado de la puerta.* - There's a window to the side of the door.

- Enfrente de/a – in front of, opposite

    a. *Ella está enfrente del escenario.* - She's in front of the stage.

- Alrededor de – around

    a. *El cochecoche pasa alrededor del parque.* - The car passes around the park.

- Encima de – on top of, above

    a. *El gato está encima de la cama.* - The cat is on top of the bed.

- Cerca de – near

    a. *Vosotros estáis cerca del museo.* - You are near the museum.

- Dentro de – inside, in, within

    a. *Rafael está dentro de la piscina.* - Rafael is in the pool.

- A pesar de - despite

    a. *Yo me mudé a pesar de los problemas.* - I moved away despite the problems.

- De acuerdo con/a – in accordance with/according to,

    a. *Tú ganaste de acuerdo con las reglas.* - You won according to the rules.

<u>Examples:</u>

1. Me gusta el pollo además de la carne.

   I like chicken as well as meat.

2. El banco está enfrente del cine.

   The bank is in front of the cinema.

3. Peter vive cerca de Jenny.

   Peter lives near Jenny.

4. Tengo galletas frescas dentro de esta bolsa.

   I have fresh cookies inside this bag.

5. Mariana se va a graduar a pesar de las dificultades.

   Mariana is going to graduate despite the difficulties.

Exercises:

1. Underline the preposition in the following sentences.

    a. Este camino lleva hasta la playa.

    b. Yo no puedo vivir sin ti.

    c. Nosotros estamos trabajando contra el reloj.

    d. Las respuestas están enfrente de ti.

    e. El tesoro se encuentra dentro de un cofre.

    f. ¿Quieres ir con mi hermano?

    g. Ellas tuvieron un buen día a pesar del mal tiempo.

    h. Mi sándwich favorito es de jamón y queso.

    i. La profesora dejó el libro sobre la mesa.

    j. España se encuentra cerca de Francia.

2. Write a preposition in Spanish to complete the sentences.

    a. Emily hizo la declaración _____ juramento.

    b. La farmacia está _____ banco.

    c. Yo me encuentro _____ una obra de arte.

    d. Sigue esta dirección _____ llegar al parque.

    e. Esta es una película _____ pingüinos.

    f. A Jorge no le gusta trabajar _____ Manuel.

    g. Debbie es amable _____ divertida.

    h. Daniel compró rosas _____ su novia.

    i. ¿Qué vas a hacer _____ las vacaciones?

    j. A Ángel no le gusta la pizza _____ piña.

3. Pick the accurate translation for each preposition.

    a. Desde

        i. Because of

        ii. Since

    b. Cerca de

        i. Near

        ii. Without

    c. Hacia

        i. Towards

        ii. Around of

    d. A pesar de

        i. Against

        ii. Despite

    e. Para

        i. Beside

        ii. For

    f. Junto a

        i. Next to

        ii. Below

    g. Ante

        i. Above of

        ii. In the face of

    h. Sin

        i. At

        ii. Without

    i. Además de

        i. Inside

        ii. As well as

    j. Encima de

        i. On top of

        ii. As far as

4. Organize the following sentences into the correct order:

    a. desde – español – un – yo – año – estudio – hace

    _____

    b. la – mi – junto a – escuela – casa – está

    _____

    c. amigos – con – yo – trabajo – mis

    _____

    d. ti – quiero – yo – sin – ir – no

    _____

    e. encima del – gato – un – techo – hay

    _____

    f. año – dentro de – yo – un – me – gradúo

    _____

    g. impostor – nosotros – hay – entre – un

    _____

    h. Patricia – Miranda – al lado de – está – siempre

    _____

    i. rosas – es – de – este – ramo – un

    _____

    j. mi – de acuerdo a – es – madre – así

    _____

5. Mark with an ✕ or ✓ if the sentences make logical sense or not:

    a. El teatro está durante el parque.   _____

    b. Mi libro se trata bajo mi vida.   _____

    c. David llegó a tiempo a pesar del tráfico.   _____

    d. No quiero pelear además de ti.   _____

    e. La clase termina dentro de una hora.   _____

    f. Mi abuelo vive en Perú.   _____

    g. ¿Quieres ir sin la playa?   _____

    h. Esta es un pastel de chocolate.   _____

    i. Andrea se fue a su casa.   _____

    j. La universidad está sobre aquí.   _____

Translations:

Translate the following sentences into English:

1. Esta es una pelea de todos contra todos.

   _____

2. El planeta Tierra gira alrededor del sol.

   _____

3. Valerie está trabajando hacia sus grandes sueños.

   _____

4. Mipadre padre dejó las llaves encima de la mesa.

   _____

5. Andrea no quiere viajar sin su gato.

   _____

6. Tu cuarto está al lado del cuarto de tu hermano.

   _____

7. Nosotros nos encontramos en tiempos difíciles.

   _____

8. Elena no trabaja bien bajo presión.

   _____

9. Este secreto debe quedar entre nosotros.

   _____

10. La ventana está junto a la puerta.

    _____

Story:

Desde que era un niño, Victor ama los **videojuegos**. Durante años, Victor ha podido pasar **horas** jugando enfrente de una **pantalla**. Le gustan todos los tipos de juegos, desde los de **deportes** hasta los de aventuras, desde los clásicos hasta los más nuevos. Sin embargo, los videojuegos le traían algunos problemas. Sus padres se quejaban de que Victor pasaba demasiado tiempo junto a sus juegos, sin salir de su **habitación**. Además, no le iba muy bien en el colegio. Hasta que un día, todo cambió. A Victor se le ocurrió que algún día podría trabajar **creando** juegos como los que tanto amaba.

Desde ese día, Victor se dedicó a **seguir** sus sueños. Nunca se detuvo, a pesar de los obstáculos en su camino. Estudió mucho, aprendió todo lo necesario, y se esforzó hasta alcanzar sus metas. Victor se encontró ante las puertas de una gran compañía. Empezó a trabajar para esa compañía de videojuegos. Victor creó juegos de acción y de estrategia, de habilidad y de simulación. Otra vez se encontró **sumergido** en su obsesión por los videojuegos. Hasta que un día, mientras diseñaba un juego sobre crear tus propios juegos, Victor se preguntó a sí mismo '¿Es posible que yo sea solo un **personaje** más de un juego?' Por muchos juegos que siguió creando, nunca consiguió responder esa importante **pregunta**.

Vocabulary List:

1. videojuegos - video games
2. horas - hours
3. pantalla - screen
4. deportes - sports
5. habitación - bedroom
6. creando - creating
7. seguir - to follow
8. sumergido - submerged
9. personaje - character
10. pregunta - question

Translated Story:

Since he was a child, Victor has loved **video games**. For years, Victor could spend **hours** in front of a **screen** playing games. He likes all types of games, from **sports** to adventure games, from the classics to the newest. However, video games brought him some problems. His parents complained that Victor spent too much time with his games, without leaving his **bedroom**. Besides, he was not doing very well in school. Until one day, everything changed. It occurred to Victor that one day he could work **creating** games like the ones he loved so much.

From that day on, Victor dedicated himself to **follow**ing his dreams. He never stopped, despite the obstacles in his way. He studied hard, learned everything he needed, and worked hard to achieve his goals. Victor found himself at the doors of a great company. He started working for this video game company. Victor created games of action and strategy, skill, and simulation. Once again, he found himself **submerged** in his obsession with video games. Until one day, while designing a game about creating your own games, Victor asked himself, 'Is it possible that I'm just one more **character** in a game?' For many games that he continued to create, he never managed to answer that important **question**.

Questions:

1. ¿Desde cuándo ama Victor los videojuegos? _____
   Since when does Victor love videogames?

2. ¿Qué le causaba problemas a Victor? _____
   What caused Victor problems?

3. ¿Cómo le iba a Victor en el colegio? _____
   How was Victor doing in school?

4. ¿Qué había en el camino de Victor hacia sus sueños? _____
   What was in Victor's way to his dreams?

5. ¿Dónde trabajaba Victor? _____
   Where did Victor work?

6. ¿En qué estaba sumergido Victor? _____
   What was Victor submerged in?

Answers:

1.

    a. Hasta

    b. Sin

    c. Contra

    d. Enfrente de

    e. Dentro de

    f. Con

    g. A pesar del

    h. De

    i. Sobre

    j. Cerca de

2.

    a. Bajo

    b. Junto al/al lado del/cerca del

    c. Ante

    d. Hasta

    e. Sobre

    f. Con

    g. Además de

    h. Para

    i. Durante

    j. Con

3.

    a. Since

    b. Near

    c. Towards

    d. Despite

    e. For

    f. Next to

g. In the face of

h. Without

i. As well as

j. On top of

4.

    a. Yo estudio español desde hace un año.

    b. La escuela está junto a mi casa.

    c. Yo trabajo con mis amigos.

    d. Yo no quiero ir sin ti.

    e. Encima del techo hay un gato/Hay un gato encima del techo.

    f. Yo me gradúo dentro de un año.

    g. Hay un impostor entre nosotros.

    h. Patricia siempre está al lado de Miranda.

    i. Este es un ramo de rosas.

    j. Así es, de acuerdo a mi madre.

5.

    a. ✗

    b. ✗

    c. ✓

    d. ✗

    e. ✓

    f. ✓

    g. ✗

    h. ✓

    i. ✓

    j. ✗

Translations:

1. This is a fight of everyone against everyone.
2. The planet Earth turns around the sun.
3. Valerie is working towards her big dreams.
4. My dad left his keys on top of the table.
5. Andrea doesn't want to travel without her cat.
6. Your room is beside your brother's room.
7. We find ourselves in difficult times.
8. Elena doesn't work well under pressure.
9. This secret must stay between us.
10. The window is next to the door.

Story:

1. Desde que era un niño.
2. Los videojuegos.
3. No muy bien.
4. Obstáculos.
5. En una compañía de videojuegos.
6. En su obsesión por los videojuegos.

Chapter 3
ADVERBS OF TIME

As you probably know, adverbs are little words that give additional meaning to the verbs of a sentence. Adverbs of time, in particular, will give information about when or how often an action takes place. This includes the duration of the action, the frequency of it, or the exact moment when it happens. They are a very important part of a sentence's structure because they will give readers or listeners the necessary context to understand when something happens.

In Spanish, these are called *adverbios de tiempo*. They are used to reply to questions like "¿Cuándo?", "¿Qué tan seguido?", y "¿En qué momento?" They can be quite specific or not, can be placed before or after the verb, and can be combined with adjectives, nouns, and verbs. It might seem like a lot to take in, but the key is to practice very often and try to immerse yourself in the Spanish language.

In the meantime, to get you started on dominating the use of adverbs of time in Spanish, we have prepared a list of all the most common adverbs of time you will need to understand to start speaking this new language fluently.

- Ahora – now

  o *Yo estoy estudiando ahora.* - I am studying now.

- Anoche – last night

  o *Ellas fueron a la fiesta anoche.* - They went to the party last night.

- Antes – before

  o *Tú comiste antes de salir.* - You ate before going out.

- Ayer – yesterday

  o *Mauricio fue al doctor ayer.* - Mauricio went to the doctor yesterday.

- Después – after

    o *Nosotros descansamos después de la clase.* - We rested after the class.

- Hoy – today

    o *Usted va a trabajar todo el día hoy.* - You are going to work the entire day today.

- Jamás/Nunca – never

    o *Ellos nunca van a la playa.* - They never go to the beach.

- Luego – after

    o *Tú vas a trabajar después de estudiar.* - You are going to work after studying.

- Mañana – tomorrow

    o *Ustedes van a viajar mañana.* - You are going to travel tomorrow.

- Pronto – soon

    o *Nosotros nos vamos a ver pronto.* - We are going to see each other soon.

- Siempre – always

    o *Mi padrepadre siempre está trabajando.* - My dad is always working.

- Tarde – late

    o *Yo me desperté tarde.* - I woke up late.

- Temprano – early

    o *La oficina abre temprano.* - The office opens early.

- Todavía/aún – still

    o *Ellos aún no se casan.* - They still haven't got married.

- Ya – already

    o *Cecilia ya se graduó.* - Cecilia already graduated.

<u>Examples:</u>

1. Hay que ir al hospital ahora.

    We have to go to the hospital now.

2. Yo pinté mi casa ayer.

    I painted my house yesterday.

3. Las vacaciones van a llegar pronto.

    The vacations are going to arrive soon.

4. Laura llega tarde al trabajo.

    Laura arrives late at work.

5. José va a ir al banco mañana.

    José is going to go to the bank tomorrow.

Additionally, as we mentioned before, sometimes adverbs specifically relate to frequency. They can be combined with other words and take on a different meaning. Here are some other useful ways in which adverbs of frequency work:

- A menudo – often

    o *Usted visita a su abuela a menudo.* - You visit your grandmother often.

- De nuevo – again

    o *Yo voy a viajar de nuevo.* - I am going to travel again.

- De pronto/de repente – suddenly

    o *De pronto empezó a llover.* - Suddenly, it started to rain.

- A veces – sometimes

    o *Nosotros cocinamos pasta a veces.* - We sometimes cook pasta.

- De día/noche – in the day/at night

  - *Mi tío trabaja de noche.* - My uncle works at night.

- Por la mañana/tarde/noche – in the morning/afternoon/at night

  - *Ellas van a estudiar por la tarde.* - They are going to study in the afternoon.

- Al amanecer/anochecer/atardecer – at dawn/nightfall/dusk

  - *Él se durmió al anochecer.* - He fell asleep at nightfall.

- Otra vez – once more/again

  - *Caterina enfermó otra vez.* - Caterina got sick again.

- En (año/mes) – in (year/month)

  - *Ellos se conocieron en diciembre.* - They met in December.

- El (día de la semana) – on (day of the week)

  - *Yo voy a renunciar el miércoles.* - I am going to quit on Wednesday.

- A las (hora) – at (specific time)

  - *Tú vas a salir a las seis.* - You are going to go out at six.

<u>Examples:</u>

1. Andrés empieza a trabajar al amanecer.
   Andrés begins working at dawn.

2. Mi tío va a la piscina a menudo.
   My uncle goes to the pool often.

3. De repente quiero comer pizza.
   Suddenly I want to eat pizza.

4. La pareja se encontró el viernes.
   The couple met on Friday.

5. A veces olvido hacer los debereslos deberes.
   Sometimes I forget to do the homework.

Exercises:

1. Choose the correct translation for each adverb of time:

   a. Anoche

   b. Todavía

   c. A veces

   d. Tarde

   e. De pronto

   f. Otra vez

   g. Hoy

   h. De día

   i. Pronto

   j. Al amanecer

   k. Suddenly

   l. Late

   m. At dawn

   n. Last night

   o. Soon

   p. In the day

   q. Sometimes

   r. Still

   s. Today

   t. Once again

2. Underline the adverbs of time in each sentence:

   a. No me molestes ahora.

   b. Hoy me desperté temprano.

   c. Fernando visita mi casa a menudo.

   d. Mañana no hay clases.

   e. De repente empezó a llover.

   f. El perro ladra de día y de noche.

   g. Yo ya llegué al hotel.

   h. ¿Tú nunca has visto esta película?

   i. El partido de fútbol fue ayer.

   j. Las brujas salen al anochecer.

3. Choose the correct adverb of time in each case:

   a. Yo llegué muy _____. (mañana/temprano)

   b. El sol sale _____. (por la mañana/al atardecer)

   c. Ella juega al tenis _____ (todavía/desde) los cinco años.

   d. ¿Quieres ir al cine _____(ayer/mañana)?

   e. El doctor te puede ver _____. (por la tarde/antes)

   f. ¿Qué quieres hacer _____ (a menudo/ahora)?

   g. (A veces/pronto) _____empiezo mi trabajo nuevo.

   h. Gabriel tiene que terminar los deberes _____. (otra vez/hoy)

i. ¿Qué soñaste _____ (anoche/al atardecer)?

j. (A veces/tarde) _____ comemos pasta en la cena.

4. Pick the right translation for each adverb of frequency:

    a. Hoy

        i. Often

        ii. Today

    b. De pronto

        i. Once more

        ii. Suddenly

    c. Jamás

        i. Never

        ii. At dusk

    d. Todavía

        i. Early

        ii. Still

    e. A veces

        i. Suddenly

        ii. Sometimes

    f. Otra vez

        i. In the night

        ii. Once more

    g. Temprano

        i. Tomorrow

        ii. Early

    h. Después

        i. After

        ii. Before

    i. De nuevo

        i. Again

        ii. Often

    j. Por la mañana

        i. In the night

ii. In the morning

5. Select an adverb of frequency to answer the following questions:

    a. When does the sun go down?

        i. Temprano

        ii. Al atardecer

    b. The day after today is …

        i. Mañana

        ii. Ayer

    c. Responsible people arrive …

        i. Tarde

        ii. Temprano

    d. When do ghosts come out?

        i. De noche

        ii. De día

    e. What do we call the night before today?

        i. Antes

        ii. Anoche

    f. When do stars come out?

        i. Al amanecer

        ii. Al anochecer

    g. How often do we have to keep breathing?

        i. Siempre

        ii. Nunca

    h. How often does it rain?

        i. Jamás

        ii. A veces

    i. When are you answering this question?

        i. Hoy

        ii. Ayer

    j. When do roosters crow?

        i. Pronto

        ii. Al amanecer

Translations:

Translate the following sentences into English:

1. Voy a ir a tu casa después de desayunar.

   _____

2. Jenny todavía no ha aprendido a hablar español.

   _____

3. Yo trabajo de día, y Lucy trabaja de noche.

   _____

4. Mi madre ya compró los regalos de navidad.

   _____

5. Juan tuvo una pesadilla anoche.

   _____

6. Los estudiantes hicieron el examen de nuevo.

   _____

7. Los niños deben estudiar antes de jugar.

   _____

8. Voy a pasear al perro y luego voy a trabajar.

   _____

9. ¿Quieres ver esta película otra vez?

   _____

10. ¿A dónde vas a ir en Junio?

    _____

Story:

En el mundo existen todo tipo de **trabajos**. Algunos son difíciles, otros son **aburridos**, y existen otros que son fascinantes. Existen también trabajos que son un poco raros, o al menos muy específicos. Tal es el caso de Matt, un **escritor** profesional que se dedica especialmente a escribir biografías de personas famosas. Matt siempre se sorprende con las cosas que **aprende** sobre estas personas. Hay músicos que se presentan en estadios y a menudo visitan pequeñas escuelas de música. Hay grandes atletas que nunca aprendieron a ir en bicicleta. Matt ya conoce todas las historias más interesantes, **divertidas**, o inspiradoras.

Por ejemplo, en 2015, Matt escribió la biografía de una **actriz**. Así descubrió que antes de ser actriz, ella había estudiado Medicina. **Sorprendentemente**, esta actriz a menudo atendía emergencias médicas de sus **compañeros** de reparto en las películas. Matt le preguntó si de día era actriz y de noche era doctora, como una superheroína. La actriz respondió que no era así, pero que pronto, si se llegaba a quedar sin trabajo como actriz, no dudaría en **volver** a los hospitales. Después de tanto éxito y tanta fama, ella todavía se interesaba por **ayudar** a los demás.

Vocabulary List:

1. trabajos - jobs
2. aburridos - boring
3. escritor - writer
4. aprende - learn
5. divertidas - funny
6. actriz - actress
7. sorprendentemente - surprisingly
8. compañeros - partners
9. volver - to return
10. ayudar – helping (to help)

Translated Story:

There are all kinds of **jobs** in the world. Some are difficult, some are **boring**, and there are others that are fascinating. There are also jobs that are a bit weird or at least very specific. Such is the case with Matt, a professional **writer** who is especially dedicated to writing the biographies of famous people. Matt is always amazed at the things he **learns** about these people. There are musicians who perform in stadiums and often visit small music schools. There are great athletes who never learned to ride a bicycle. Matt already knows all the most interesting, **funny**, or inspiring stories.

For example, in 2015, Matt wrote the biography of an **actress**. Thus he discovered that before being an actress, she had studied medicine. **Surprisingly**, this actress often treated medical emergencies for her **partners** in the cast of the movies. Matt asked her if she was an actress during the day and if she was a doctor at night, like a superhero. The actress replied that she was not like that. But that soon, if she were to lose her job as an actress, she would not hesitate to **return** to the hospitals. After so much success and fame, she still cared about **helping** others.

Questions:

1. ¿Cuál es el trabajo de Matt? _____
   What is Matt's job?

2. ¿Sobre quién escribe Matt? _____
   Who does Matt write about?

3. ¿Sobre quién escribió Matt en 2015? _____
   Who did Matt write about in 2015?

4. ¿Quiénes tenían emergencias médicas? _____
   Who had medical emergencies?

5. ¿Qué le interesaba a la actriz? _____
   What interested the actress?

6. ¿A dónde volvería la actriz sin dudarlo? _____
   Where would the actress return to without a doubt?

Answers:

1.

     a. Last night

     b. Still

     c. Sometimes

     d. Late

     e. Suddenly

     f. Once again

     g. Today

     h. In the day

     i. Soon

     j. At dawn

2.

     a. Ahora

     b. Temprano

     c. A menudo

     d. Mañana

     e. De repente

     f. De día y de noche

     g. Ya

     h. Nunca

     i. Ayer

     j. Al anochecer

3.

     a. Temprano

     b. Por la mañana

     c. Desde

     d. Mañana

e. Por la tarde

f. Ahora

g. Pronto

h. Hoy

i. Anoche

j. A veces

4.

a. Today

b. Suddenly

c. Never

d. Still

e. Sometimes

f. Once more

g. Early

h. After

i. Again

j. In the morning

5.

a. Al atardecer

b. Mañana

c. Temprano

d. De noche

e. Anoche

f. Al anochecer

g. Siempre

h. A veces

i. Hoy

j. Al amanecer

Translations:

1. I am going to go to your house after breakfast.

2. Jenny still hasn't learned to speak Spanish.

3. I work in the day, and Lucy works in the night.

4. My mom already bought the Christmas gifts.

5. Juan had a nightmare last night.

6. The students did the exam again.

7. The children should study before playing.

8. I am going to walk the dog and after, I am going to work.

9. Do you want to watch this movie again?

10. Where are you going to go in June?

Story:

1. Escritor profesional.

2. Personas famosas.

3. Una actriz.

4. Los compañeros de reparto.

5. Ayudar a los demás.

6. A los hospitales.

Chapter 4
REFLEXIVE VERBS

When we talk about reflexive verbs, we are talking about those cases when the subject and the object refer to the same. This means the subject of the sentence is doing something to themselves. In English, for example, we can say, "I dress myself." Now we are going to study this kind of sentence in Spanish.

Generally, reflexive verbs are more common in Spanish than in English. They can be identified by the addition of "-se" to the infinitive form of the verb. For example, we have the verb "vestir," which, as a reflexive verb, would be "vestirse." The translation would be "to dress oneself," which could be simplified to mean "to get dressed." Here we include a list of essential reflexive verbs everyone should know in Spanish:

- Acostarse – to go to bed

    o *Él va a acostarse.* - He is going to go to bed.

- Bañarse – to take a bath

    o *El gato no quiere bañarse.* - The cat doesn't want to take a bath.

- Despertarse - to wake up

    o *Ella tiene que despertarse temprano.* - She has to wake up early.

- Enfadarse – to get angry

    o *Mis padres van a enfadarse.* - My parents are going to get angry.

- Llamarse – to be called

    o *El bebé va a llamarse Simón.* - The baby is going to be called Simón.

- Levantarse – to get up

    o *Usted tiene que levantarse de la silla.* - You have to get up from the chair.

- Reírse – to laugh

- *Mis hermanos van a reírse de la película.* - My brothers are going to laugh at the movie.

- Sentarse – to sit down

  - *Vosotros os tenéis que sentar.* - You have to sit down.

- Verse – to see

  - *La niña no puede verse en el espejo.* - The girl can't see herself in the mirror.

- Vestirse – to get dressed

  - *Los bebés no pueden vestirse solos.* - Babies can't dress themselves alone.

Examples:

1. Es hora de acostarse.
   It's time to go to bed.

2. No hay necesidad de enfadarse.
   There's no need to get angry.

3. Es buen momento para reírse.
   It's a good moment to laugh.

Now, to conjugate reflexive verbs and form entire sentences, you will need to take a look at the following table:

Person	Singular Pronouns	Plural Pronouns
First Person	**Me** (matches with **yo**)	**Nos** (matches with **nosotros/as**)
Second Person	**Te** (matches with **tú**) OR **Se** (matches with **usted**)	**Os** (matches with **vosotros/as**)
Third Person	**Se** (matches with **él** or **ella**)	**Se** (matches with **ellos** or **ellas**)

In this case, you don't have to add "-se" to the verbs. The sentence would be structured this way: "Yo me visto." (I dress myself). Instead of "Yo me vestirse," which would be incorrect. First, the noun, second, the pronoun, and third, the reflexive verb conjugated. In fact, the noun can be omitted, leaving just "Me visto" as a valid sentence to indicate "I dress myself."

Here's a different example for each pronoun to illustrate how it is done:

- *Yo me visto muy bien.* - I dress very well.
- *Tú te llamas como tu abuela.* - You are named after your grandmother.
- *Usted se despierta al amanecer.* - You wake up at sunrise.
- *Él se sienta en el suelo.* - He sits on the floor.
- *Nos reímos mucho juntos.* - We laugh a lot together.
- *Vosotros os enfadáis muy fácilmente.* - You get angry very easily.
- *Ellos se acuestan muy tarde.* - They go to bed very late.

Examples:

1. Él se baña.

    He takes a bath.

2. Nosotros nos vemos.

    We see each other.

3. Carla se levanta.

    Carla gets up.

Exercises:

1. Transform the following verbs into reflexive verbs:

    a. Calmar _____

    b. Lavar _____

    c. Duchar _____

    d. Peinar _____

    e. Hablar _____

    f. Afeitar _____

    g. Sacar _____

    h. Escribir _____

    i. Secar _____

    j. Comprar _____

2. Underline all the reflexive verbs in each sentence:

    a. Yo me llamo Manuela.

    b. Victoria se viste muy elegante.

    c. Mis hermanos se acuestan muy tarde.

    d. A veces, Simón se corta mientras se afeita.

    e. Los domingos nosotros no nos despertarnos temprano.

    f. Esta es una nueva forma de peinarse.

    g. Mi padre quiere comprarse unos pantalones.

    h. La modelo se ve en el espejo.

    i. ¿Tú te despiertas a las 8?

    j. No hay que reírse de la tragedia.

3. Take the conjugated reflexive verbs and write them in their original form with the termination "-se":

    a. Vemos _____

    b. Cantamos _____

    c. Pinta _____

    d. Caen _____

    e. Despierto _____

f. Sientan _____

g. Lastimas _____

h. Sube _____

i. Levantamos _____

j. Cortas _____

4. Convert these English verbs into reflexive verbs in Spanish:

    a. Scare _____

    b. Tire _____

    c. Sell _____

    d. Paint _____

    e. Cut _____

    f. Read _____

    g. Listen _____

    h. Move _____

    i. Jump _____

    j. Eat _____

5. Match the options on the left with the correct conjugation on the right:

    a. Nosotros + Verse   k. Se hablan

    b. Ella + Enfadarse   l. Se ríe

    c. Mario + Reírse   m. Nos vemos

    d. Yo + Comprar   n. Se llaman

    e. Jenny + Calmar   o. Se calma

    f. Ellos + Hablarse   p. Nos compramos

    g. Ustedes + Llamarse   q. Se saltan

    h. Nosotros + Comprar   r. Se enfada

    i. Ellas + Saltarse   s. Te comes

    j. Tú + Comerse   t. Me compro

Translations:

Translate the following sentences into English:

1. Yo me levanto temprano todos los días.

    _____

2. Mi tía no puede parar de reírse.

    _____

3. Todos tenemos que calmarnos un poco.

    _____

4. Mi equipo se llama los Tigres.

    _____

5. Mi hijo aprendió a vestirse.

    _____

6. Isabel y Luisa se ven todos los viernes.

    _____

7. Yo me enfado con mi padre.

    _____

8. Tú tienes que peinarte el cabello.

    _____

9. Ustedes no pueden sentarse ahí.

    _____

10. Ellos se compran ropa nueva en diciembre.

    _____

Story:

Amnesia. Se trata de la **pérdida** total o parcial de la memoria. La amnesia hace que no podamos **recordar** un suceso o un periodo de nuestras vidas. La amnesia puede ser causada por un accidente o algún trauma. Es algo que puede o no tener cura. Todos hemos escuchado acerca de la amnesia en algún u otro momento. Pero yo nunca pensé que me pasaría a mí. Yo me desperté un día en una **cama** de un hospital, y no tenía ni idea de cómo había llegado hasta ahí. Mientras esperaba a que algún doctor o **enfermera** se diera cuenta de que yo estaba despierto, intenté recordar qué me había pasado

Primero, traté de recordar mi **infancia**. Y me alegré al darme cuenta de que lo recordaba todo. Recuerdo cuando me caí de mi primera bicicleta. Recuerdo cuando mi perro se escapó de la casa. Recuerdo también cuando empecé el colegio, los nombres de mis amigos, los **chistes** que aún nos contamos. Pero no puedo recordar nada de lo que pasó antes de que yo llegara al hospital. No sé a qué hora me desperté. No sé si me bañé. No sé si fui a trabajar. No sé qué me pasó.

Finalmente, un doctor entra a mi habitación y sonríe **tímidamente** mientras me explica: "Es muy poco probable que esto pase, pero hoy te cayó un **rayo** durante una **tormenta**. De acuerdo con nuestros exámenes, estás **sano**, pero seguro nunca olvidarás este increíble evento."

Vocabulary List:

1. pérdida - loss
2. recordar - to remember
3. cama - bed
4. enfermera - nurse
5. infancia - childhood
6. chistes - jokes
7. tímidamente - shyly
8. rayo - lighting
9. tormenta - storm
10. sano - healthy

Translated Story:

Amnesia. It is about the total or partial **loss** of memory. Amnesia makes us unable to **remember** an event or a period in our lives. Amnesia can be caused by an accident or some trauma. It is something that may or may not have a cure. We have all heard of amnesia at some point or another. But I never thought it would happen to me. I woke up one day in a hospital **bed**, and had no idea how I got there. While waiting for some doctor or **nurse** to realize that I was awake, I tried to remember what had happened to me?

First, I tried to remember my **childhood**. And I was glad to realize that I remembered everything. I remember when I fell off my first bike. I remember when my dog ran away from the house. I also remember when I started school, the names of my friends, and the **jokes** that we still tell each other. But I can't remember anything that happened before I got to the hospital. I don't know what time I woke up. I don't know if I bathed. I don't know if I went to work. I do not know what happened to me.

Finally, a doctor walks into my room and smiles **shyly** as he explains. "This is highly unlikely to happen, but you were struck by **lightning** today during a **storm**. According to our examinations, you are **healthy**, but you will surely never forget this incredible event." I think he thought it was kind of funny.

Questions:

1. ¿De qué se trata la amnesia? _____

   What is amnesia about?

2. ¿Qué cosas pueden causar amnesia? _____

   What things can cause amnesia?

3. ¿Dónde se despertó el personaje del cuento? _____

   Where did the character from the story wake up?

4. ¿De dónde se cayó el personaje del cuento? _____

   Where did the character in the story fall from?

5. ¿Quién se escapó de la casa? _____

   Who ran away from home?

6. ¿Qué le cayó al personaje del cuento? _____

   What struck the character from the story?

Answers:

1.

       a.   Calmarse

       b.   Lavarse

       c.   Ducharse

       d.   Peinarse

       e.   Hablarse

       f.   Afeitarse

       g.   Sacarse

       h.   Escribirse

       i.   Secarse

       j.   Comprarse

2.

       a.   Me llamo

       b.   Se viste

       c.   Se acuestan

       d.   Se corta + se afeita

       e.   Nos despertamos

       f.   Peinarse

       g.   Comprarse

       h.   Se ve

       i.   Te despiertas

       j.   Reírse

3.

       a.   Verse

       b.   Cantarse

       c.   Pintarse

       d.   Caerse

       e.   Despertarse

       f.   Sentarse

g. Lastimarse

h. Subirse

i. Levantarse

j. Cortarse

4.

a. Asustarse

b. Cansarse

c. Venderse

d. Pintarse

e. Cortarse

f. Leerse

g. Escucharse

h. Moverse

i. Saltarse

j. Comerse

5.

a. Nosotros + Verse - m. Nos vemos

b. Ella + Enfadarse - r. Se enfada

c. Mario + Reírse - l. Se ríe

d. Yo + Comprar - t. Me compro

e. Jenny + Calmar - o. Se calma

f. Ellos + Hablarse - k. Se hablan

g. Ustedes + Llamarse - n. Se llaman

h. Nosotros + Comprar - p. Nos compramos

i. Ellas + Saltarse - q. Se saltan

Translations:

1. I get up early every day.

2. My aunt can't stop laughing.

3. We all have to calm down a little.

4. My team is called the Tigers.

5. My son learned how to dress himself.

6. Isabel and Luisa see each other every Friday.

7. I get angry with my dad.

8. You have to brush your hair.

9. You can't sit there.

10. They buy themselves new clothes in December.

Story:

1. Pérdida total o parcial de la memoria.

2. Un accidente o algún trauma.

3. En una cama de un hospital.

4. De su primera bicicleta.

5. Un perro.

6. Un rayo.

Chapter 5
SABER AND CONOCER

In this chapter, we are going to study the Spanish verbs "Saber" and "Conocer." These are important verbs to study carefully because they can be a little confusing. The reason is that in English, both of these verbs are translated as "to know," but in Spanish, they are used for different cases. It's very important to know the difference so that you are aware of when to use each verb.

The verb "Saber" is used in reference to information or skills you may or may not have. For example, the time, the date, languages, talents, etc.

The verb "Conocer" is used to talk about familiarity with things, people, or places. For example, friends, celebrities, locations, cities, etc.

Here you will find a useful chart to see the way Saber and Conocer are conjugated with different nouns to form a sentence:

Person	Saber	Conocer
Yo	sé	conozco
Tú	sabes	conoces
Él/Ella	sabe	conoce
Nosotros/as	sabemos	conocemos
Vosotros/as	sabéis	conocéis
Ellos/as	saben	conocen

Examples:

1. ¿Tú sabes qué día es hoy?

   Do you know what day today is?

2. Ella no me conoce.

She doesn't know me.

3. Yo sé nadar.

   I know how to swim.

4. Ellos conocen el mejor restaurante de la ciudad.

   They know the best restaurant in the city.

5. ¿Vosotras sabéis hablar francés?

   Do you know how to speak French?

6. Yo conozco muy bien Ontario en Canadá.

   I am very familiar with Ontario in Canada.

Exercises:

1. Identify if these English sentences would refer to the verbs "Saber" or "Conocer":

    a. She knows when my birthday is.   _____

    b. We know Madrid well.   _____

    c. The teacher isn't familiar with Mexico.   _____

    d. Elias knows karate.   _____

    e. ¿Do you know Selena Gomez?   _____

    f. ¿How long have you known him?   _____

    g. My dog knows how to play fetch.   _____

    h. I am familiar with that restaurant.   _____

    i. You don't know the hotel's manager.   _____

    j. Martha knows how to play the flute.   _____

2. Conjugate "Saber" or "Conocer" in the appropriate way to match each requirement:

    a. Yo + Saber   _____

    b. Tú + Conocer   _____

    c. Nosotros + Conocer   _____

    d. Carla + Saber   _____

    e. Vosotros + Saber   _____

    f. Mis abuelos + Conocer   _____

    g. Ángel + Saber   _____

    h. Él + Conocer   _____

    i. Mis primos + Saber   _____

    j. Tú + Saber   _____

3. Write a ✓ or a ✗ to indicate if the sentence is written correctly or not:

    a. Yo no conozco a Penélope Cruz.   _____

    b. Tú sabes Estados Unidos.   _____

    c. ¿Conoces a mi novia?   _____

    d. Él no sabe esta tienda de ropa.   _____

    e. Elizabeth conoce bailar muy bien.   _____

    f. Yo quiero saber Japón.   _____

g. Yo sé que día es hoy. _____

h. ¿Conoces jugar hockey? _____

i. Ellas saben hablar alemán. _____

j. Vosotros no conocen mi casa. _____

4. Conjugate the verb "Saber" or "Conocer" appropriately in the following sentences:

   a. Mi hermano _____ ese parque. (conocer, mi hermano)

   b. Rafael _____ hablar seis idiomas. (saber, Rafael)

   c. ¿_____ a Rita Moreno? (conocer, tú)

   d. Yo no _____ bailar tango. (saber, yo)

   e. Luisa _____ cocinar comida italiana. (saber, Luisa)

   f. ¿Quieres _____ a mi gato? (conocer, tú)

   g. Vosotros _____ que fecha es hoy. (saber, vosotros)

   h. Mis tíos _____ el estadio de fútbol. (conocer, mis tíos)

   i. Tú _____ Río de Janeiro. (conocer, tú)

   j. Él _____ tocar esta canción. (saber, él)

5. Complete the following sentences with the verb "Saber" or "Conocer" according to which fits each sentence:

   a. Mi hijo ya _____ leer.

   b. Yo no _____ la Torre Eiffel.

   c. ¿Tú _____ al profesor de español?

   d. Mariana no _____ nadar.

   e. ¿Tú _____ hablar italiano?

   f. Nosotros _____ la mejor playa del país.

   g. Tú _____ a mi esposo.

   h. Ella no _____ que día es hoy.

   i. ¿Quién _____ qué hora es?

   j. Lola _____ a la escritora del libro.

Translations:

Translate the following sentences into English:

1. Martha sabe hablar cinco idiomas.

_____

2. ¿Sabes dónde está mi hermana?

_____

3. Nosotros sabemos las respuestas del examen.

_____

4. ¿Vosotros conocéis al profesor Rafael?

_____

5. Él sabe jugar al fútbol americano.

_____

6. Yo no conozco Bélgica todavía.

_____

7. Mi padrepadre conoce a un buen doctor.

_____

8. Ella sabe cantar y bailar muy bien.

_____

9. Francisco no conoce a mi mejor amiga.

_____

10. ¿Tú sabes cómo abrir esta caja?

_____

Story:

Todas las personas somos diferentes. Todas nuestras vidas son diferentes. Hay algo muy especial en lo que todos somos únicos: los **sueños**. Nuestros grandes sueños son algo muy especial. Las **metas** que tenemos pueden definir nuestras vidas enteras. Desde que somos niños, soñamos a lo grande. Muchos niños desean ser superhéroes o princesas. Pero también hay niños que sueñan con ser doctores o **bomberos**, y estos niños persiguen sus sueños, se esfuerzan, trabajan duro, y logran **alcanzar** sus metas en la vida. También hay casos en los que los sueños cambian. Por ejemplo, cuando yo tenía cinco años quería ser una profesora. Luego soñé con ser **abogada**, chef, e incluso directora de cine. Esto es normal. Pero ¿qué pasa cuando llegamos a cierta edad sin alcanzar nuestros sueños?

Yo empecé la universidad a los diecisiete años. Yo estudié Medicina durante dos años. Aprendí mucho, pero ¡era muy difícil! Dejé de estudiar un par de años para trabajar y **ahorrar** dinero. En ese tiempo también aprendí mucho. Ahora sé cocinar, **limpiar**, **vender**, y **cuidar** niños. Ahora conozco más partes de la ciudad, conozco personas muy interesantes, y me conozco mejor a mí misma. Estas experiencias me enseñaron mucho. Pero aún no sé cuál es mi gran sueño en la vida. Sin embargo, aprendí algo aún más importante. Todos somos diferentes, y no hay una sola forma de vivir la vida. Tú puedes seguir un gran sueño, puedes seguir muchos sueños, o puedes disfrutar cada **etapa** de vida y aprender todo lo que puedas.

Vocabulary List:

1. sueños - dreams
2. metas - goals
3. bomberos - firefighters
4. alcanzar – to reach
5. abogada - lawyer
6. ahorrar - to save
7. limpiar - to clean
8. vender - to sell
9. cuidar - to take care of
10. etapa - stage

Translated Story:

All the people are different. All of our lives are different. There is something very special in which we are all unique: **dreams**. Our big dreams are something very special. The **goals** we have can define our entire life. Since we are children, we dream big. Many children wish they were superheroes or princesses. But there are also children who dream of being doctors or **firefighters**, and these children pursue their dreams, they try hard, they work hard, and they **reach** their goals in life. There are also cases where dreams change. For example, when I was five I wanted to be a teacher. Then I dreamed of being a **lawyer**, a chef, and even a film director. This is normal. But what happens when we reach a certain age without reaching our dreams?

I started college at seventeen. I studied medicine for two years. I learned a lot, but it was very difficult! I stopped studying for a couple of years to work and **save** money. In that time I also learned a lot. Now I know how to cook, **clean**, **sell**, and **take care of** kids. Now I know more parts of the city, I know very interesting people, and I know myself better. These experiences taught me a lot. But I still don't know what my big dream in life is. However, I learned something even more important. We are all different, and there is no one way to live life. You can follow a great dream, you can follow many dreams, or you can enjoy each **stage** of life and learn everything you can.

Questions:

1. ¿Qué hacemos cuando somos niños? _____

   What do we do when we're children?

2. ¿Qué quería ser la narradora a los cinco años? _____

   What did the narrator want to be at five years old?

3. ¿Qué hizo la narradora a los diecisiete años? _____

   What did the narrator do at seventeen years old?

4. ¿Qué estudió la narradora durante dos años? _____
   ____

   What did the narrator study for two years?

5. ¿Qué cosas sabe hacer la narradora? _____

   What things does the narrator know how to do?

6. ¿Qué cosas conoce la narradora? _____

   What things does the narrator know?

Answers:

1.

      a. Saber

      b. Conocer

      c. Conocer

      d. Saber

      e. Conocer

      f. Conocer

      g. Saber

      h. Conocer

      i. Conocer

      j. Saber

2.

      a. Yo sé

      b. Tú conoces

      c. Nosotros conocemos

      d. Carla sabe

      e. Vosotros sabéis

      f. Mis abuelos conocen

      g. Ángel sabe

      h. Él conoce

      i. Mis primos saben

      j. Tú sabes

3.

      a. ✓

      b. ✗

      c. ✓

      d. ✗

      e. ✗

f. ✗

g. ✓

h. ✗

i. ✓

j. ✓

4.

    a. Conoce

    b. Sabe

    c. Conoces

    d. Sé

    e. Sabe

    f. Conocer

    g. Saben

    h. Conocen

    i. Conoces

    j. Sabe

5.

    a. Sabe

    b. Conozco

    c. Conoces

    d. Sabe

    e. Sabes

    f. Conocemos

    g. Conoces

    h. Sabe

    i. Sabe

    j. Conoce

Translations:

1. Martha knows how to speak five languages.
2. Do you know where my sister is?
3. We know the answers of the exam.
4. Do you know Professor Rafael?
5. He know how to play American Football.
6. I don't know Belgium yet/I am not familiar with Belgium yet.
7. My dad knows a good doctor.
8. She knows how to sing and dance very well.
9. Francisco doesn't know my best friend.
10. Do you know how to open up this box?

Story:

1. Soñamos a lo grande.
2. Una profesora.
3. Empezó la universidad.
4. Medicina.
5. Cocinar, limpiar, vender, y cuidar niños.
6. Más partes de la ciudad, personas muy interesantes, y a sí misma.

Chapter 6
EMOTIONS AND PAIN

A key part of successfully carrying out full conversations in Spanish is to learn how to express how you feel. Emotions are something universal, and it's important to know how to put them into words in every new language we learn. In this chapter, we will teach you the question used in Spanish to inquire about a person's emotions or health, the most commonly used phrases to express yourself, and finally, some ways to explain feelings of pain.

As always, it's important to remember a few essential things about the Spanish language. When you speak Spanish, the form of adjectives will change depending on the gender of the person. In this case, for example, to say someone is scared, the masculine form is *asustado*, while the female form is *asustada*.

Additionally, it's important to remember the way *Ser y Estar* work in Spanish. Many emotions can be used both ways, but there are a few differences to be aware of, and the verb *Tener* is also sometimes used. For example, you can be nervous (*estar nervioso*), or you can have nerves (*tener nervios*). Here are a few examples of this particular case:

- Be nervous/Have nerves - Estar nervioso/Tener nervios
- Be hungry/Have hunger - Estar hambriento/Tener hambre
- Be thirsty/Have thirst - Estar sediento/Tener sed
- Be scared/Have fear - Estar asustado/Tener miedo
- Be in pain/Have pain - Estar adolorido/Tener dolor
- Be hot - Estar acalorado/Tener calor
- Be sleepy - Estar soñoliento/Tener sueño

Because the verb *Ser* is very important and complex, there is an additional way to use it; when one of these adjectives is used to describe a person as part of their personality. In English, you can say, "I am happy." In Spanish, you can say "Estoy feliz" to indicate you are currently experiencing a feeling of happiness, or you can say "Soy feliz" to express that you are a happy person. This refers to something more general than the current moment.

Here are some examples to understand this:

- Yo soy una persona muy divertida. - I am a very funny person.

- El profesor es muy aburrido. - The teacher is very boring.

- Ella es una persona triste. - She is a sad person.

- Nosotros somos muy nerviosos. - We are very nervous.

- Usted es alguien cansado. - You are somebody who is tired.

Now, let's learn how to ask about the emotions or state of a person.

- How are you? - ¿Cómo estás?

- How have you been? - ¿Cómo has estado?

- How do you feel? - ¿Cómo te sientes?

- What is happening to you? - ¿Qué te pasa?

- What do you feel? - ¿Qué sientes?

- What is hurting you? - ¿Qué te duele?

Next, we will include a list of the most common feelings and emotions that you will need while practicing your Spanish.

- Sad - Triste

- Happy - Feliz

- Angry - Enfadado/a, Molesto/a

- Excited - Emocionado/a

- Bored - Aburrido/a

- Surprised - Sorprendido/a

- Worried - Preocupado/a

- Scared - Asustado/a

- Confused - Confundido/a

- Tired - Cansado/a

- In love - Enamorado/a

The verb *Estar* can be used in sentences like this: *Subject* + Verb *Estar* (estoy, estás, está, estamos, están) + a feeling or emotion. Take a look at the following examples:

- Yo estoy feliz de verte. - I am happy to see you.

- Mi madre está muy triste hoy. - My mom is very sad today.

- Nosotros estamos emocionados de ir a la playa. - We are excited about going to the beach.

- Usted está asustado porque hay tormenta. - You are scared because there's a storm.

- Él está enamorado por primera vez. - He is in love for the first time.

- Ellas están confundidas sobre los deberes. - They are confused about the homework.

- Tú estás muy aburrido en tu trabajo. - You are very bored in your job.

This is an extensive subject in every language, so it's useful to know as many ways as possible to put your emotions into words. For this reason, we will teach you how to express how you feel about a subject.

- I like it. - Me gusta.

- I dislike it. - No me gusta.

- I love it. - Me encanta./Lo amo.

- I hate it. - Lo odio.

That's not all. There's an optional but frequently used addition to these sentences. In this case the structure would be, for example: **A + (mí, ti, él, ella, usted, nosotros/as, ellos, ellas, vosotros/as) + me gusta.**

- A mí me gusta la música.

- A ti te gusta la comida italiana.

- A él le gusta bailar salsa.

- A nosotros no nos gusta el inglés.

- A vosotros no os gusta esta clase.

If this sounds a little difficult, there's no need to worry. We'll review and dive deeper into this subject in **Chapter 8**. So make sure you learn the basics here and feel encouraged to return to this lesson once you've mastered the subject.

Finally, it's vital to be aware of how to express pain or discomfort. It could be lifesaving knowledge. So here you can learn the most important phrases for it.

- I'm in pain. - Yo tengo dolor.

- That hurts. - Eso duele.

- It's bleeding. - Está sangrando.

- It's broken. - Está roto.

- It's hurt. - Está herido.

- Headache - Dolor de cabeza
- Stomachache - Dolor de estómago
- Chest pain - Dolor de pecho

Examples:

1. Manuel está preocupado por el examen.
   Manuel is worried about the exam.

2. Mi hermana tiene mucha sed.
   My sister is very thirsty.

3. Esta película me hace sentir triste.
   This movie makes me feel sad.

4. Jorge se despertó con dolor de cabeza.
   Jorge woke up with a headache.

5. Odio el café.
   I hate coffee.

Exercises:

1. Underline the emotion expressed in each sentence:

    a. Mi madre ha estado muy preocupada.

    b. Los hermanos se sienten felices juntos.

    c. ¿Estás asustado?

    d. Hoy me desperté sediento.

    e. Mi mejor amiga está enamorada.

    f. ¿Por qué estás enfadada?

    g. Al perro le duele una pata.

    h. José está muy cansado.

    i. Ella dice que no está confundida.

    j. ¿Quién los sorprendió?

2. Connect the questions with the fitting answers:

a. ¿Cómo estás?	1. Sí, me duele la cabeza.
b. ¿Qué te duele?	2. No, no está aburrido.
c. ¿Te duele la cabeza?	3. No, se rompió un brazo.
d. ¿Te sangra la nariz?	4. No, no me duele la garganta.
e. ¿Nico se rompió una pierna?	5. Sí, tengo mucha hambre.
f. ¿Judy tiene dolor de estómago?	6. Me duelen los pies.
g. ¿Te duele la garganta?	7. Le tengo miedo a la oscuridad.
h. ¿Tienes mucha hambre?	8. Sí, le duele el estómago.
i. ¿Él está aburrido?	9. No, no está sangrando.
j. ¿A qué le tienes miedo?	10. Estoy bien, gracias.

3. Pick the correct way to answer each question:

    a. ¿Tienes frío?

        i. Sí, sí tengo.

        ii. No, no duele.

    b. ¿Estás cansada?

        i. No, no puedo.

        ii. No, no lo estoy.

c. ¿Tienes dolor de pecho?

    i. Sí, sí está.

    ii. Sí, sí tengo.

d. ¿Qué te duele?

    i. Me duele la cabeza.

    ii. Está sangrando.

e. ¿Cómo estás?

    i. Estoy adolorida.

    ii. Estoy en mi casa.

f. ¿Quién está preocupado?

    i. Yo tengo calor.

    ii. Mi tío está preocupado.

g. ¿Qué se rompió?

    i. La pierna.

    ii. Dolor de pecho.

h. ¿Está sangrando mucho?

    i. Sí, mucha sed.

    ii. Sí, mucho.

i. ¿Te sientes triste?

    i. Sí, muy aburrido.

    ii. No, estoy feliz.

j. ¿Te gusta esta canción?

    i. Sí, me duele.

    ii. Sí, me gusta.

4. Use a ✓ or a ✗ to mark the sentences that make sense or don't make sense:

a. Me da miedo el lunes.   _____

b. Por la noche tengo mucha hambre.   _____

c. ¿Te duele mucha sangre?   _____

d. Me gusta mucho esta diez.   _____

e. Mi tío está muy feliz hoy.   _____

f. ¿El día está adolorido?   _____

g. Luisa tiene dolor de cabeza.   _____

h. Mis hijas están aburridas en clase.   _____

i. ¿No te gusta la sopa?   _____

j. En invierno tengo mucho estoy.   _____

5. Circle the correct word in each case:

   a. Cuando tengo hambre, tengo que: comer / beber

   b. En verano hace mucho: dolor / calor

   c. Una herida: sangra / rompe

   d. Mi primo está: sueño / asustado

   e. Este libro: cansado / me gusta

   f. El clima frío: no me gusta / está herido

   g. Rosa tiene un brazo: feliz / roto

   h. El ejercicio te deja: confundido / cansado

   i. La cabeza: me duele / me gusta

   j. Tengo dolor de: pecho / feliz

Translations:

Translate the following sentences into English:

1. No me gusta el alcohol; me da dolor de cabeza.

   _____

2. Cathy se siente muy feliz de estar aquí.

   _____

3. Mi primo está enamorado por primera vez.

   _____

4. ¿Cómo has estado? Espero que te sientas mejor.

   _____

5. ¡Ayuda! Mi brazo está roto.

   _____

6. Nosotros estamos muy cansados después del viaje.

   _____

7. Él nunca se aburre en la clase de historia.

   _____

8. Andrés va a ir al hospital porque su nariz está sangrando.

   _____

9. ¿Qué sientes? ¿Tienes dolor de pecho?

   _____

10. No tengas miedo; todo va a estar bien.

    _____

Story:

Este lunes, los estudiantes tuvieron una clase muy importante. La profesora de historia les habló a los estudiantes sobre las cosas que nos hacen humanos. Es decir, las cosas que nos **separan** de los animales, las cosas que marcaron el **inicio** de la civilización en la historia. Por tal motivo, los estudiantes **revisaron** momentos importantes de la historia de la humanidad. Cuando el ser humano siente hambre, aprende a **cazar**, a **pescar**, a **sembrar** alimentos y a cocinarlos en el fuego. Cuando las personas sienten frío, aprenden a construir viviendas, a coser ropa, y mantener el fuego. Cuando las familias crecen y se unen entre sí, se convierten en pueblos y en ciudades, luego en reinos y finalmente en países.

Pero se mantiene la pregunta, ¿qué es lo que nos hace humanos? ¿qué nos diferencia de los animales? ¿qué evento marca el inicio de la civilización? Los estudiantes tenían algunas ideas. Ellos nombraron el arte, la **guerra**, la **paz**, el lenguaje, y la historia. Pero la profesora compartió con sus estudiantes una teoría muy especial que los conmovió a todos. **Según** la profesora, existe la teoría de que el inicio de la civilización lo marca un hueso roto que tuvo tiempo de **sanar**. Esto significa que existió una persona con compasión que acompañó y cuidó a la persona herida hasta que sanó. Eso es lo que nos hace humanos.

Vocabulary List:

1. separan - separate
2. inicio - beginning
3. revisaron - reviewed
4. cazar - to hunt
5. pescar - to fish
6. sembrar - to plant
7. guerra - war
8. paz - peace
9. según - according to
10. sanar - to heal

Translated Story:

This Monday, the students had a very important class. The history teacher talked to the students about the things that make us human. That is, the things that **separate** us from the animals, the things that marked the **beginning** of civilization in history. For this reason, the students **reviewed** important moments in the history of mankind. When a human being feels hungry, he learns to **hunt**, **fish**, **plant** food, and cook it in a fire. When people feel cold, they learn to build houses, sew clothes, and keep a fire. As families grow and join together, they become towns and cities, then kingdoms, and finally, countries.

But the question remains, what makes us human? What differentiates us from animals? What event marks the beginning of civilization? The students had some ideas. They named art, **war**, **peace**, language, and history. But the teacher shared with her students a very special theory that moved them all. **According** to the teacher, there is a theory that the beginning of civilization is marked by a broken bone that she had time to **heal**. This means that there was a compassionate person who accompanied and nursed the injured person back to health. That is what makes us human.

Questions:

1. ¿Qué pasó el lunes? _____

   What happened on Monday?

2. ¿Sobre qué habló la profesora? _____

   What did the teacher talk about?

3. ¿Qué hacen los seres humanos cuando tienen hambre? _____

   _____

   What do humans do when they are hungry?

4. ¿Qué ideas tenían los estudiantes? _____

   What ideas did the students have?

5. ¿Qué pasa cuando las familias crecen y se unen? _____

   _____

   What happens when families grow and get together?

6. ¿Qué le pasó al hueso roto? _____

   What happened to the broken bone?

Answers:

1.

      a. preocupada

      b. felices

      c. asustado

      d. sediento

      e. enamorada

      f. enojada

      g. duele

      h. cansado

      i. confundida

      j. sorprendió

2.

      a. a-10

      b. b-6

      c. c-1

      d. d-9

      e. e-3

      f. f-8

      g. g-4

      h. h-5

      i. i-2

      j. j-7

3.

      a. i

      b. ii

      c. ii

      d. i

      e. i

      f. ii

g. i

h. ii

i. ii

j. ii

4.

    a. ✗

    b. ✓

    c. ✗

    d. ✗

    e. ✓

    f. ✗

    g. ✓

    h. ✓

    i. ✓

    j. ✗

5.

    a. comer

    b. calor

    c. sangra

    d. asustado

    e. me gusta

    f. no me gusta

    g. roto

    h. cansado

    i. me duele

    j. pecho

Translations:

1. I don't like alcohol; it gives me a headache.

2. Cathy is very happy to be here.

3. My cousin is in love for the first time.

4. How have you been? I hope you feel better.

5. Help! My arm is broken.

6. We are very tired after the trip.

7. He never gets bored in history class.

8. Andres is going to the hospital because his nose is bleeding.

9. What do you feel? Do you have chest pains?

10. Don't be scared; everything will be fine.

Story:

1. Los estudiantes tuvieron una clase muy importante.

2. Sobre las cosas que nos hacen humanos.

3. Cazar, pescar, sembrar alimentos y cocinarlos en el fuego.

4. Se convierten en pueblos y en ciudades, luego en reinos y finalmente en países.

5. El arte, la guerra, la paz, el lenguaje y la historia.

6. El hueso roto sanó.

Chapter 7
OBLIGATIONS AND WISHES

¿Quieres aprender español? Then you have a lot to study. By now, you probably know the basics about using the words *querer* and *necesitar*. However, it isn't as simple as it seems. There's a lot of additional information you'll need to express obligations and wishes properly in Spanish. It's important to review a few expressions very closely.

We will start with two ways to talk about obligations - things you *have to* do. First, we have "tener." While this word in Spanish might be translated to *"own,"* when you say "tener que," that means something you *"have to do."* Before the examples, here's the correct way to use the verb:

Person	Present	Past	Future
Yo	tengo que	tuve que	tendré que
Tú	tienes que	tuviste que	tendrás que
Él/Ella/	tiene que	tuvo que	tendrá que
Nosotros/as	tenemos que	tuvimos que	tendremos que
Vosotros/as	tenéis que	tuvisteis que	tendreis que
Ellos/as	tienen que	tuvieron que	tendrán que

Examples:

1. Yo tendré que ir a clase el lunes.

   I will have to go to go class on Monday.

2. Tú tienes que hacer ejercicio todos los días.

   You have to exercise every day.

3. Él tuvo que llamar a la policía.

   He had to call the police.

88

4. Ella tendrá que comprar otro coche.

   She will have to buy another car.

5. Nosotros tenemos que permanecer unidos.

   We have to stay together.

6. Vosotros tenéis que dejaros de pelear.

   You have to stop fighting.

7. Ellos tuvieron que mudarse a otro país.

   They had to move to another country.

8. Ellas tendrán que estudiar juntas.

   They will have to study together.

Then there is the second expression, and this one is a little different. When there is "something" that "has to" be done, in Spanish, you can say "hay que." This way, there is no need to specify who is doing the deed. In other words, there is no need to include a subject in the sentence. The correct way is to say "Hay que" + something that needs to be done.

Examples:

1. Hay que limpiar toda la casa.

   One has to clean the entire house.

2. Hay que alimentar a las mascotas.

   One has to feed the pets.

3. Hay que tratar bien a los vecinos.

   One has to treat the neighbors well.

4. Hay que ser positivos.

One has to be positive.

5. Hay que seguir buscando una solución.

   One has to keep looking for a solution.

6. Hay que tener paciencia con los niños.

   One has to be patient with children.

Next, it is time to review in detail how to put your needs, desires, and wishes into Spanish. There are two main words you'll need to learn how to use: "querer" and "necesitar." These two verbs mean "want" and "need," respectively. In general terms, "querer" is used when there's something you'd like to have, do, or be. Meanwhile, "necesitar" is kept for more vital or stronger wishes. To illustrate this point, we will show how to use these two words and give some examples before diving straight into the exercises.

Person	Querer	Necesitar
Yo	quiero	necesito
Tú	quieres	necesitas
Él/Ella	quiere	necesita
Nosotros/as	queremos	necesitamos
Vosotros/as	queréis	necesitáis
Ellos/as	quieren	necesitan

Examples:

1. Él quiere aprender a nadar.

   He wants to learn how to swim.

2. Mis abuelos quieren ir a la playa.

My grandparents want to go to the beach.

3. Nosotros necesitamos comprar comida.

    We need to buy food.

4. Fabiana necesita un abrazo.

    Fabiana needs a hug.

5. Yo quiero viajar en barco.

    I want to travel by ship.

6. Tú necesitas ir al hospital.

    You need to go to the hospital.

Exercises:

1. Fill in the blanks with "querer" or "necesitar" according to each case:

   a. Los seres vivos _____ oxígeno para vivir.

   b. Yo _____ salir a bailar esta noche.

   c. ¿Tú _____ un doctor?

   d. Javi _____ comprar una casa nueva.

   e. ¿Tú _____ ir a la fiesta conmigo?

   f. Yo _____ estos ingredientes para cocinar.

   g. Los peces _____ una pecera.

   h. Los niños _____ ir al zoológico.

   i. Yo no _____ un novio.

   j. ¿Vosotros _____ ayuda con eso?

2. Complete the sentence with the appropriate words from the other column:

   a. _____ tienen que ir a clase.   1. Las aves

   b. _____ tienen que aprender a caminar.   2. Los estudiantes

   c. _____ tienen que escuchar a los dueños.   3. Los músicos

   d. _____ tienen que aguantar el frío.   4. Los exploradores

   e. _____ tienen que ser valientes.   5. Los bomberos

   f. _____ tienen que vivir en el agua.   6. Los restaurantes

   g. _____ tienen que saber volar.   7. Los niños pequeños

   h. _____ tienen que practicar mucho.   8. Los perros

   i. _____ tienen que viajar mucho.   9. Los pingüinos

   j. _____ tienen que abrir los domingos.   10. Los peces

3. Fill in the blanks with "tener que" or "hay que" according to each case:

   a. Los domingos _____ ir a misa.

   b. Mi tío _____ arreglar el coche.

   c. ¿Ella _____ irse temprano?

   d. _____ dormir ocho horas diarias.

   e. Elizabeth _____ leer este libro.

   f. No _____ perder la calma.

g. Sebastián _____ buscar un trabajo.

h. Los jugadores _____ ir al Campeonato.

i. ¿Yo también _____ comer ensalada?

j. _____ seguir las reglas del juego.

4. Complete the sentences by circling the verb that matches the first part of the sentence:

a. Si tienes hambre, tú tienes que: comer / lavar

b. Si tiene sed, él tiene que: beber / correr

c. Si tenemos sueño, tenemos que: caminar / dormir

d. Si está sucio, al coche hay que: quemarlo / lavarlo

e. Si hay música, hay que: dormir / cantar

f. Si hay problemas, tenemos que: hablar / conducir

g. Si estamos en la playa, tenemos que: volar / nadar

h. Si van a la discoteca, tienen que: bailar / viajar

i. Si quieren aprender, ellos tienen que: cantar / estudiar

j. Si quiero saber más, yo tengo que: leer / cocinar

5. Mark the following statements as true or false:

a. Los tiburones tienen que saber volar.   _____

b. Hay que viajar al sol.   _____

c. Todos necesitamos un amigo.   _____

d. El televisor necesita electricidad.   _____

e. Las mascotas no necesitan amor.   _____

f. Los jueces tienen que ser honestos.   _____

g. Hay que cuidar a los abuelos.   _____

h. No hay que proteger a los niños.   _____

i. Todas las mujeres necesitan un hombre.   _____

j. El helado necesita estar frío.   _____

Translations:

Translate the following sentences into English:

1. Mi compañero necesita ayuda médica.

_____

2. ¿Necesitas ir al baño urgentemente?

_____

3. ¿Qué quieres para Navidad este año?

_____

4. El equipo de fútbol necesita practicar mucho más.

_____

5. Yo creo que tú necesitas un descanso.

_____

6. Mi primo necesita ayuda para hacer los deberes.

_____

7. ¿Vosotros necesitáis algo para comer o beber?

_____

8. Ella quiere que se acabe la guerra.

_____

9. Pablo quiere ser bombero cuando sea grande.

_____

10. Las dos mujeres quieren pedir helado de chocolate.

_____

Story:

Cada vez que **despega** una nueva nave espacial, todo el planeta lo celebra. Todos sabemos cuándo un nuevo astronauta viaja al espacio. Es algo muy emocionante, es un momento único en la historia. Sin embargo, a veces hay historias secretas detrás de estos grandes momentos. A veces, no nos **enteramos** de las cosas más interesantes. Es posible que las historias más fascinantes pasen aquí, en nuestro planeta, en los laboratorios de los **científicos**.

Para empezar, construir una **nave espacial** no es nada fácil. Antes que nada, los científicos tienen que estudiar durante muchos años. Hay que saber mucho sobre mecánica, **física**, el espacio, y otros planetas. Luego, hay que llevar a cabo muchos experimentos muy interesantes. La nave espacial tiene que ser muy fuerte: no se puede romper, ni explotar. Los **trajes** de los astronautas tienen que ser muy seguros: no se pueden dañar, ni dejar que los astronautas se pierdan flotando en el espacio.

Estas son lecciones muy importantes. En el proceso, es posible que las naves de **prueba** exploten, se desmonten, o incluso se derritan. Así como los astronautas, mientras se preparan, se pueden asustar, **desmayar**, o **vomitar**. De estas experiencias nacen las historias más divertidas e **inesperadas** que el resto del mundo aún no conoce.

Vocabulary List:

1. despega - take off
2. enteramos - find out
3. científicos - scientists
4. nave espacial - spaceship
5. física - physics
6. traje - suit
7. prueba - test
8. desmayarse - to faint
9. vomitar - to throw up
10. inesperadas - unexpected

Translated Story:

Every time a new spaceship **takes off**, the entire planet celebrates. We all know when a new astronaut travels to space. It is something very exciting; it is a unique moment in history. However, sometimes there are secret stories behind these big moments. Sometimes, we don't **find out** about the most interesting things. It is possible that the most fascinating stories happen here on our planet, in the laboratories of the **scientists**.

To begin with, building a **spaceship** is not easy at all. First of all, scientists have to study for many years. One has to know a lot about mechanics, **physics**, space, and other planets. Then, one has to do many very interesting experiments. The spaceship has to be very strong; it can't break or explode. The **suits** of the astronauts have to be very safe; they can't get ruined, nor let the astronauts get lost floating in space.

These lessons are very important. In the process, it is possible that the **test** ships explode, break down, or even melt down. Just as the astronauts, while they prepare themselves, they can get scared, **faint**, or **throw up**. From these experiences are born the most fun and **unexpected** stories that the rest of the world doesn't know yet.

Questions:

1. ¿Qué celebra todo el planeta? _____

   What does the entire planet celebrate?

2. ¿Qué hay detrás de estos grandes momentos? _____

   What is behind these big moments?

3. ¿Dónde pasan las historias más interesantes? _____

   Where do the most exciting stories happen?

4. ¿Qué es lo primero que tienen que hacer los científicos? _____

   What is the first thing that scientists have to do?

5. ¿Qué le puede pasar a los astronautas si sus trajes no son seguros? _____

   _____

   What could happen to the astronauts if their suits aren't safe?

6. ¿Qué es lo que el resto del mundo no conoce? _____

   What does the rest of the world not know?

Answers:

1.

    a. necesitan

    b. quiero

    c. necesitas

    d. quiere

    e. quieres

    f. necesito

    g. necesitan

    h. quieren

    i. quiero/necesito

    j. necesitáis/queréis

2.

    a. Los estudiantes

    b. Los niños pequeños

    c. Los perros

    d. Los pingüinos

    e. Los bomberos

    f. Los peces

    g. Las aves

    h. Los músicos

    i. Los exploradores

    j. Los restaurantes

3.

    a. hay que

    b. tiene que

    c. tiene que

    d. hay que

    e. tiene que

    f. hay que

g. tiene que

h. tienen que

i. tengo que

j. hay que

4.

a. comer

b. beber

c. dormir

d. lavar

e. cantar

f. hablar

g. nadar

h. bailar

i. estudiar

j. leer

5.

a. false

b. false

c. true

d. true

e. false

f. true

g. true

h. false

i. false

j. true

Translations:

1. Mi partner needs medical help.

2. Do you need to go to the bathroom urgently?

3. What do you want for Christmas this year?

4. The soccer team needs to practice a lot more.

5. I think you need a break.

6. My cousin needs help to do the homework.

7. Do you need something to eat or drink?

8. She wants the war to be over.

9. Pablo wants to be a firefighter when he grows up.

10. The two women want to order chocolate ice cream.

Story:

1. Que despega una nave espacial.

2. Historias secretas.

3. En nuestro planeta, en los laboratorios.

4. Estudiar durante muchos años.

5. Se pueden perder flotando en el espacio.

6. Las historias más divertidas e inesperadas.

Chapter 8
GUSTAR AND SIMILAR VERBS

¿Te gusta el español? Did you know there are many different ways to say you like something? In this wonderful language, there are a great number of verbs that can be used to describe how you feel about a certain thing. And, of course, this also includes the things you might not like.

To build this kind of sentence, you will need to use the following formula: ***Indirect Object Pronoun* + gustar (or similar verb) + subject.**

Remember, the Indirect Object Pronouns are *me, nos, te, le,* and *les.* And *gustar,* or the verb you choose, must be conjugated to match the subject, meaning that if it is a single subject, you will use *gusta,* and if it is a plural subject, the correct way is to say *gustan.* The same will be done with other verbs, taking the *r* at the end of the infinitive for a singular subject and replacing it with an *n* for plural subjects.

Person	(Optional)	(Add for negative sentences)	Indirect Object Pronoun	(Nouns in singular or verbs)	(Nouns in plural)
I	a mí		me		
You	a ti		te		
He, She, It	a él, ella,	(no)	le	gusta	gustan
We	a nosotros		nos		
You	a vosotros/as		os		
They	a ellos/as		les		

Although you'll notice that part of the sentence is optional, it's actually very commonly used, as we'll see in the following examples. Here are the most used verbs to express positive and negative feelings, plus a few examples.

- Gustar – To like

  - A mí me gusta ir al cine. (I like going to the movie theater.)

  - No te gusta la pizza con jamón. (You don't like pizza with ham.)

- Encantar – To love

  - A él no le encantan las montañas rusas. (He doesn't love rollercoasters.)

  - Nos encanta ir a este restaurante los viernes. (We love to go to this restaurant on Fridays.)

- Atraer – To attract

  - A ella le atrae el olor de las rosas. (She is attracted by the smell of roses.)

  - Les atraen las personas divertidas. (They are attracted by funny people.)

- Fascinar – To fascinate

  - A ti te fascinan las películas de acción. (You are fascinated by action movies.)

  - Me fascinan todos los tipos de insectos. (I am fascinated by all types of insects.)

- Interesar – To interest

  - A nosotros no nos interesa la historia antigua. (We are not interested in ancient history.)

  - Le interesan las artes marciales. (He's interested in martial arts.)

- Disgustar – To dislike/be upset by

  - A ellos les disgusta la comida picante. (They dislike spicy food.)

  - Le disgustan las personas con malos modales. (She dislikes people with bad manners.)

- Molestar – To bother

  - A mí no me molesta el clima lluvioso. (I am not bothered by rainy weather.)

  - Nos molesta que cantes esta canción. (We are bothered by you singing this song.)

- Aburrir – To bore

o A ti te aburre leer este libro. (You are bored of reading this book.)

o Les aburre esperar el bus cada mañana. (They're bored of waiting for the bus each morning.)

<u>Examples:</u>

1. A mí me gusta la música instrumental.
   I like instrumental music.

2. A mi primo le interesa el espacio.
   My cousin is interested in space.

3. Nos disgustan las discusiones.
   We dislike arguments.

4. Te encantan las películas de acción.
   You love action movies.

5. Les aburren las clases de matemáticas.
   They get bored by math class.

Exercises:

1. Take the following words and write them in the correct order in a sentence:

    a. gustan - gatos - le - no - los

    _____

    b. nosotros - encanta - playa - la - nos - a

    _____

    c. libros - a - gustan - ti - los - te - románticos

    _____

    d. molesta - él - tipo - a - de - música - le - este

    _____

    e. les - concierto - aburre - el

    _____

    f. mucho - te - bailar – gusta

    _____

    g. Camila - los - le - no - animales - interesan - a

    _____

    h. no - francés - le - el - gusta

    _____

    i. atrae - nos - olor - ese

    _____

    j. a - no - avión - ellos - gusta - les - viajar - en

    _____

2. Fill in the blanks with the correct Indirect Object Pronoun for each statement:

    a. A ti _____ gustan los delfines.

    b. A ellas no _____ interesan los superhéroes.

    c. A Enrique _____ molestan los sombreros.

    d. A mí _____ encanta la pizza italiana.

    e. A mis amigos _____ atrae la ciencia ficción.

    f. A las cantantes _____ encanta su trabajo.

    g. A nosotros no _____ aburren los documentales.

    h. A mis tías _____ gusta estar en casa.

i. A Paul _____ disgusta tomar cerveza.

j. A mí no _____ molesta despertarme temprano.

3. Write the following verbs conjugated as requested:

   a. Aburrir for a plural subject: _____

   b. Gustar for a verb: _____

   c. Encantar for a plural subject: _____

   d. Molestar for a singular subject: _____

   e. Disgustar for a plural subject: _____

   f. Gustar for a singular subject: _____

   g. Fascinar for a verb: _____

   h. Atraer for a verb: _____

   i. Atraer for a singular subject: _____

   j. Interesar for a plural subject: _____

4. Translate the following sentences to Spanish using the structure as shown:

   a. I like apples.

   _____

   b. You dislike the theater.

   _____

   c. He gets bored with driving a car.

   _____

   d. We are interested in Antarctica.

   _____

   e. Stephanie loves horses.

   _____

   f. They are bothered by the winter.

   _____

   g. Mario is fascinated by the stars.

   _____

   h. I love horror movies.

   _____

i. We are upset by being hungry.

_____

j. You are attracted by learning languages.

_____

5. Correctly conjugate the verbs in each sentence:

    a. Les (gustar) _____ ir al parque.

    b. Me (encantar) _____ el color azul.

    c. Le (aburrir) _____ leer este libro.

    d. Nos (molestar) _____ los insectos en el jardín.

    e. Te (fascinar) _____ cocinar recetas nuevas.

    f. Le (atraer) _____ las tendencias de moda.

    g. Les (disgustar) _____ llegar tarde a clase.

    h. Me (gustar) _____ la camisa blanca.

    i. Nos (aburrir) _____ este edificio.

    j. Te (encantar) _____ los museos de la ciudad.

Translations:

Translate the following sentences into English:

1. Al profesor le disgustan los días lluviosos.

   _____

2. Nos encanta ir a nadar al río.

   _____

3. A ti no te gusta ver series de televisión dramáticas.

   _____

4. A Rafael le aburren los amigos de su hermana.

   _____

5. Les molestan las personas groseras.

   _____

6. Me atraen las casas de campo.

   _____

7. A los esposos les encantan las grandes fiestas.

   _____

8. A Karina le disgustan las comidas picantes.

   _____

9. Te fascina tocar la guitarra eléctrica.

   _____

10. A nosotros no nos gusta viajar fuera del país.

   _____

Story:

Es 14 de febrero, el día de San Valentín. Cuando el **jefe** de la **empresa** llega a trabajar, al salir del **ascensor** lo recibe un perro golden retriever. El perro mueve la cola y parece sonreír. Tiene una **pajarita** roja y su placa de nombre dice "Valentín." Sobre la espalda, el perro lleva sujeta una cesta llena de pequeños **regalos**, cada uno con una **tarjeta**. El jefe de la compañía encuentra **rápidamente** una tarjeta con su nombre y su chocolate favorito. El dulce gesto le causa mucha risa, pero no tiene ni idea de quién es el responsable de este acto.

El resto de los trabajadores llegan a la oficina uno a uno. Carmen recibe su tarjeta junto a una rosa azul, su favorita. Nicolás también recibe un pequeño regalo: un autógrafo de su **cantante** favorito. Fernanda se sorprende mucho con su regalo: un **llavero** que había perdido recientemente. Así, todos los empleados se fueron a casa ese día con pequeños pero significativos regalos en sus manos, y sinceras sonrisas en sus rostros. Al final del día, todos se sentían tan felices que ninguno se preguntó: ¿De dónde salió Valentín, el **mensajero** del Día de San Valentín?

Vocabulary List:

1. jefe - boss
2. empresa - company
3. ascensor - elevator
4. pajarita - bow tie
5. regalos - gifts
6. tarjeta - card
7. rápidamente - quickly
8. cantante - singer
9. llavero - keychain
10. mensajero - messenger

Translated Story:

It's February 14, Valentine's Day. When the **boss** of the **company** arrives at work, he is greeted by a golden retriever as he exits the **elevator**. The dog wags its tail and appears to be smiling. He has a red **bow tie,** and his name tag says "Valentine." On his back, the dog has a basket full of small gifts, each with a **card**. The company boss **quickly** finds a card with his name and his favorite chocolate. The sweet gesture makes him laugh a lot, but he has no idea who is responsible for this act.

The rest of the workers arrive at the office one by one. Carmen receives her card along with a blue rose, her favorite. Nicolás also receives a small gift, an autograph from his favorite **singer**. Fernanda is very surprised with her gift, a **keychain** that she had recently lost. Thus, all the employees went home that day with small but meaningful gifts in their hands and sincere smiles on their faces. At the end of the day, everyone was so happy that no one wondered where did Valentine, the **messenger** of Valentine's Day, come from?

Questions:

1. ¿Qué tiene de especial el 14 de febrero? _____

   What is special about February 14?

2. ¿Quién llega primero a la empresa? _____

   Who arrives first at the company?

3. ¿Quién usa una pajarita? _____

   Who wears a bow tie?

4. ¿Qué hay en la cesta que carga el perro? _____

   What is in the basket carried by the dog?

5. ¿Cuál es el regalo de Carmen? _____

   What is Carmen's gift?

6. ¿Cuál es el regalo de Nicolás? _____

   What is Nicolás' gift?

Answers:

1.

    a. No le gustan los gatos.

    b. A nosotros nos encanta la playa.

    c. A ti te gustan los libros románticos.

    d. A él le molesta este tipo de música.

    e. Les aburre el concierto.

    f. Te gusta bailar mucho.

    g. A Camila no le interesan los animales.

    h. No le gusta el francés.

    i. Nos atrae ese olor.

    j. A ellos no les gusta viajar en avión.

2.

    a. te

    b. les

    c. le

    d. me

    e. les

    f. les

    g. nos

    h. les

    i. le

    j. me

3.

    a. aburren

    b. gusta

    c. encantan

    d. molesta

    e. disgustan

    f. gusta

g. fascina

h. atrae

i. atrae

j. interesan

4.

a. Me gustan las manzanas.

b. Te disgusta el teatro.

c. Le aburre conducir un coche.

d. Nos interesa la Antártida.

e. A Stephanie le encantan los caballos.

f. Les molesta el invierno.

g. A Mario le fascinan las estrellas.

h. Me encantan las películas de terror.

i. Nos disgusta estar hambrientos.

j. Te atrae aprender idiomas.

5.

a. gusta

b. encanta

c. aburre

d. molestan

e. fascina

f. atraen

g. disgusta

h. gusta

i. aburre

j. encantan

Translations:

1. The professor dislikes rainy days.

2. We like to go swimming in the river.

3. You don't like to watch TV drama series.

4. Rafael gets bored by his sister's friends.

5. They are bothered by mean people.

6. I'm attracted to country houses.

7. The spouses (husband and wife) love big parties.

8. Karina dislikes spicy food.

9. You are fascinated with playing electric guitar.

10. We don't like to travel outside the country.

Story:

1. Es el día de San Valentín.

2. El jefe.

3. El perro.

4. Pequeños regalos cada uno con una tarjeta.

5. Una rosa azul.

6. Un autógrafo de su cantante favorito.

Chapter 9
PRESENT PERFECT

The present perfect in Spanish is quite similar to what we are used to in English. This type of sentence is used to express complete or finished actions, which are usually things that have happened recently. For example, *I have eaten breakfast. She has done her homework.*

In Spanish, this is called the "Pretérito perfecto." The most important thing to remember is the use of two verbs to construct a sentence. There is always the auxiliary verb "Haber" (*to have*), and then the main verb, regular or irregular, in its past tense.

First, the auxiliary verb must be conjugated appropriately.

Person	Haber
Yo	he
Tú	has
Él, Ella,	ha
Nosotros/as	hemos
Vosotros/as	habéis
Ellos/as	han

Then, in this case, the regular verbs in Spanish that end in "-ar", change to the past participle of "-ido." The ones that end in "-er" or "-ir", get the past participle "-ado." Meanwhile, irregular verbs have a unique transformation. Here are a few examples:

Regular

- Caminar - caminado

  - *Tú has caminado desde el parque.* - You have walked from the park.

- Jugar - jugado

- ○ *Nosotras hemos jugado al fútbol.* - We have played soccer.

- Cocinar - cocinado

  - ○ *Usted ha cocinado toda la comida.* - You have cooked all the food.

- Dormir - dormido

  - ○ *Mi abuelo no ha dormido en toda la noche.* - My grandfather hasn't slept all night.

- Mentir - mentido

  - ○ *Mariana ha mentido todo este tiempo.* - Mariana has lied all this time.

- Comer – comido

  - ○ *Él nunca ha comido sushi.* - He has never eaten sushi.

- Poder - podido

  - ○ *Yo no he podido hacer los deberes.* - I haven't been able to do the homework.

Irregular

- Hacer - hecho

  - ○ *Mi hermano no ha hecho el trabajo.* - My brother hasn't done the job.

- Escribir - escrito

  - ○ *Vosotros habéis escrito algo hermoso.* - You have written something beautiful.

- Decir - dicho

  - ○ *La profesora ha dicho las instrucciones.* - The teacher has said the instructions.

- Poner - puesto

  - ○ *Tú has puesto el libro aquí.* - You have put the book here.

- Ver - visto

o *Daniel ha visto esta película muchas veces.* - Daniel has seen this movie many times.

Examples:

1. Teresa ha escrito una novela.

   Teresa has written a novel.

2. Yo no he podido leer el libro.

   I haven't managed to read the book.

3. Nosotros hemos visto la película de nuevo.

   We have seen the movie again.

4. Tú has caminado por el parque.

   You have walked through the park.

5. El perro se ha comido toda su comida.

   The dog has eaten all its food.

Exercises:

1. Transform the following regular verbs using the correct past participle:

   a. Nadar _____

   b. Leer _____

   c. Correr _____

   d. Pintar _____

   e. Dibujar _____

   f. Beber _____

   g. Pedir _____

   h. Morder _____

   i. Cazar _____

   j. Lavar _____

2. Complete these sentences using the conjugation of the auxiliary verb "haber":

   a. Nosotros _____ vuelto a casa.

   b. El gato _____ roto el sofá.

   c. Ella _____ descubierto un tesoro.

   d. Yo _____ resuelto el problema.

   e. Vosotros no _____ dicho nada hoy.

   f. Las plantas no _____ muerto todavía.

   g. Tony _____ escrito una carta.

   h. Ellos _____ visto un robo.

   i. Nosotros no _____ puesto música.

   j. Fátima _____ hecho un gran trabajo.

3. Indicate if the following verbs in past tense are regular or irregular:

   a. Cosido _____

   b. Plantado _____

   c. Muerto _____

   d. Bañado _____

   e. Dejado _____

   f. Satisfecho _____

g. Devuelto   _____

h. Marcado   _____

i. Besado   _____

j. Abierto   _____

4. Complete these sentences with the past tense of the verb in parenthesis:

   a. Vosotros habéis (llegar) _____ justo a tiempo.

   b. Ella no ha (dormir) _____ en toda la noche.

   c. Maribel ha (decir) _____ una mentira.

   d. Los animales han (escapar) _____ del zoológico.

   e. Yo no he (hacer) _____ esto solo.

   f. Mis hermanos han (llegar) _____ temprano.

   g. Tú has (poner) _____ la mesa.

   h. Él ha (abrir) _____ la tienda.

   i. El villano ha (morir) _____ en el libro.

   j. Nosotros hemos (pintar) _____ la casa.

5. Pick the correct option for the past tense of the following verbs:

   a. Escribir

      i. Escrito

      ii. Escribido

   b. Leer

      i. Leído

      ii. Leida

   c. Ver

      i. Veida

      ii. Visto

   d. Sentar

      i. Senticho

      ii. Sentado

   e. Resolver

      i. Resolvido

      ii. Resuelto

118

f. Correr

      i. Corrido

      ii. Corrida

g. Hacer

      i. Hacido

      ii. Hecho

h. Bailar

      i. Bailido

      ii. Bailado

i. Despertar

      i. Despertado

      ii. Despertido

j. Poder

      i. Podicho

      ii. Podido

Translations:

Translate the following sentences into English:

1. Gabriel no ha vuelto a la playa.

_____

2. ¿Tú has visitado a tu abuelo?

_____

3. Mis amigos han bailado toda la noche.

_____

4. Mi novia aún no ha visto mi película favorita.

_____

5. Yo no he podido llegar a tiempo al trabajo.

_____

6. Félix ha pedido ayuda para completar los deberes.

_____

7. Mi padre ha dicho que está muy casado esta tarde.

_____

8. Nosotros hemos corrido por todo el parque.

_____

9. Ella ha comido muy poco esta semana.

_____

10. ¿Vosotros habéis resuelto el misterio?

_____

Story:

En 2010, cuando era todavía muy **joven**, David dijo que algún día iba a **escalar** el monte Everest. Esta es la **montaña** más alta del mundo. No cualquier persona puede **cumplir** una meta como esa. No muchas personas en la historia han llegado a la cima del monte Everest. Pero David tiene un sueño. Él ha decidido hacer lo que sea necesario para cumplir su sueño. No iba a ser nada fácil. Pero lo más importante es no **rendirse** nunca.

Así empezó la historia de David. Desde ese momento, empezó a prepararse. David ha **entrenado** cada semana durante diez años. Empezó despacio pero seguro. David se dijo a sí mismo que tendría que **avanzar** cada vez un **paso** más. Así entrenó sus músculos, empezó a escalar **colinas**, paredes artificiales, y luego pequeñas montañas. A través de los años, las montañas crecieron, y David también. Cuando finalmente llegó el día, David se enfrentó a muchos **desafíos**. El monte Everest fue extremadamente difícil, pero David avanzó cada vez un paso más, y ahora puede decir que ha subido hasta la cima de la montaña más alta del mundo.

Vocabulary List:

1. joven - young
2. escalar - to climb
3. montaña - mountain
4. cumplir - to achieve
5. rendirse - to give up
6. entrenado - trained
7. avanzar - to advance
8. paso - step
9. colinas - hills
10. desafíos - challenges

Translated Story:

In 2010, when he was still very **young**, David said that one day he would **climb** Mount Everest. This is the highest **mountain** in the world. Not everyone can **achieve** a goal like that. Not many people in history have reached the top of Mount Everest. But David has a dream. He has decided to do whatever it takes to achieve his dream. It wasn't going to be easy. But the most important thing is never to **give up**.

Thus began the story of David. From that moment, he began to prepare. David has **trained** every week for ten years. He started slowly but surely. David told himself that he would have to **advance** one **step** at a time. So he trained his muscles; he began to climb **hills**, artificial walls, and then small mountains. Through the years, the mountains grew, and so did David. When the day finally came, David faced many **challenges**. Mount Everest was extremely difficult. But David took it one step at a time, and now he can say that he has climbed to the top of the highest mountain in the world.

Questions:

1. ¿Qué iba a hacer David en el monte Everest? _____

   What was David going to do on Mount Everest?

2. ¿Qué es el monte Everest? _____

   What is Mount Everest?

3. ¿Qué es lo más importante? _____

   What is the most important thing?

4. ¿Cómo entrenó David? _____

   How did David train?

5. ¿Cómo avanzó David? _____

   How did David advance?

6. ¿Cómo fue escalar el monte Everest? _____

   How was climbing Mount Everest?

Answers:

1.

    a. Nadado

    b. Leído

    c. Corrido

    d. Pintado

    e. Dibujado

    f. Bebido

    g. Pedido

    h. Mordido

    i. Cazado

    j. Lavado

2.

    a. Hemos

    b. Ha

    c. Ha

    d. He

    e. Habéis

    f. Han

    g. Ha

    h. Han

    i. Hemos

    j. Ha

3.

    a. Regular

    b. Regular

    c. Irregular

    d. Regular

    e. Regular

    f. Irregular

g. Irregular

h. Regular

i. Regular

j. Irregular

4.

   a. Llegado

   b. Dormido

   c. Dicho

   d. Escapado

   e. Hecho

   f. Llegado

   g. Puesto

   h. Abierto

   i. Muerto

   j. Pintado

5.

   a. Escrito

   b. Leído

   c. Visto

   d. Sentado

   e. Resuelto

   f. Corrido

   g. Hecho

   h. Bailado

   i. Despertado

   j. Podido

Translations:

1. Gabriel hasn't returned to the beach.

2. Have you visited your grandfather?

3. My friends have danced all night.

4. My girlfriend still hasn't seen my favorite movie.

5. I haven't managed to arrive on time at work.

6. Felix has asked for help to finish the homework.

7. My dad has said that he is very tired this afternoon.

8. We have run through all the park.

9. She has eaten very little this week.

10. Have you solved the mystery?

Story:

1. Escalar.

2. La montaña más alta del mundo.

3. Nunca rendirse.

4. Cada semana durante diez años.

5. Un paso a la vez.

6. Extremadamente difícil.

Chapter 10
IMPERATIVE

The imperative is a very important part of learning Spanish. It is something that you will notice that comes up in everyday conversation right away. The imperative is a mood used to give orders or advice and make requests, suggestions, or offer invitations.

You can often spot them as a single word between exclamation points, like "¡Help!" But they can also be arranged in more extensive sentences, like "Hagan silencio." The equivalent in English is similar - a single word used like an order or a verb preceded by the word "Let's." For example, "Move!" or "Let's move!"

To form imperative sentences, you must learn to conjugate the verbs. Firstly, you should know that the imperative isn't used in the 3rd person. So the imperative mood uses Tú (you, singular, informal), Usted (you, singular, formal), Nosotros (we), and Vosotros (you, plural).

Now, to conjugate the verbs, there are a few things to remember:

- Regular verbs ending in **-ar**: take the present tense of the verb, take off the endings (-as, -a, -amos, -an), and replace them with -a, -e, -emos, -ad.

- Regular verbs ending in **-er**: take the present tense of the verb, take off the endings (-es, -e, -emos, -en), and replace them with -e, -a, -amos, -ed.

- Regular verbs ending in **-ir**: take the present tense of the verb, take off the endings (-es, -e, -imos, -en), and replace them with -e, -a, -amos, -id.

- Irregular verbs have unique ways of conjugating the imperative form.

Here are a series of examples of how to conjugate some verbs of each kind:

Person	Regular verbs			Irregular verbs		
	Caminar	Correr	Pedir	Decir	Hacer	Ir
Tú	Camina	Corre	Pide	Di	Haz	Ve
Usted	Camine	Corra	Pida	Diga	Haga	Vaya
Nosotros	Caminemos	Corramos	Pidamos	Digamos	Hagamos	Vamos
Vosotros	Caminad	Corred	Pedid	Decid	Haced	Id

Examples:

1. Id a comer temprano.
   Go to eat early.

2. Caminemos por la playa.
   Let's walk on the beach.

3. ¡Pide ayuda!
   Ask for help!

4. Diga qué tengo que hacer.
   Say what I have to do.

5. Corre rápido.
   Run fast.

6. ¡Di la verdad!
   Tell the truth!

7. Camila, por favor, lava los platos.

Camila, please, watch the dishes.

8. Os pido que hagáis los deberes rápido.

    I ask you do the homework quickly.

9. Señor, conserve la calma.

    Sir, keep calm.

10. Ve a pasear al perro.

    Go and walk the dog.

Exercises:

1. Turn the following verbs into the imperative mood, according to the subject in parenthesis:

   a. (Tú) Abrir _____

   b. (Nosotros) Leer _____

   c. (Usted) Pintar _____

   d. (Tú) Limpiar _____

   e. (Vosotros) Lavar _____

   f. (Nosotros) Plantar _____

   g. (Usted) Dibujar _____

   h. (Tú) Decidir _____

   i. (Nosotros) Partir _____

   j. (Vosotros) Doblar _____

2. Mark with a ✓ the imperative sentences, and with a ✗ the different kind of sentences:

   a. Nadar es fácil. _____

   b. Mira la película. _____

   c. Tome un vaso de agua. _____

   d. Quiero dormir. _____

   e. Cocinad mucha comida. _____

   f. Hay que decir la verdad. _____

   g. No tengo miedo. _____

   h. Caminemos juntos. _____

   i. Dibujad algo hermoso. _____

   j. No está haciendo frío. _____

3. Fill the space in parenthesis with Tú, Usted, Nosotros, Vosotros, to fit with each sentence:

   a. (_____) Deja de hablar.

   b. (_____) Caminad en una sola fila.

   c. (_____) Diga la verdad.

   d. (_____) ¡Corre por tu vida!

   e. (_____) Bebed todo el zumo.

   f. (_____) Haz los deberes de historia.

g. (   ) ¡Ve a casa urgentemente!

h. (   ) Escuchad las instrucciones.

i. (   ) Hablemos muy seriamente.

j. (   ) Decida qué quiere comer hoy.

4. Write the infinitive form of the following irregular verbs currently in the imperative mood

    a. Siéntate   _____

    b. Muere   _____

    c. Decid   _____

    d. Estemos   _____

    e. Haz   _____

    f. Duerma   _____

    g. Probad   _____

    h. Pon   _____

    i. Salgamos   _____

    j. Seamos   _____

5. Connect both columns to form full sentences that make sense together:

    a. Camina   1. temprano esta noche.

    b. Vayamos   2. tan rápido como puedas.

    c. Escuchad   3. en la fiesta juntos.

    d. Duerme   4. permiso antes de salir.

    e. Hagamos   5. con tu mejor amigo.

    f. Pida   6. un paso cada vez.

    g. Bailad   7. juntos al cine.

    h. Corre   8. mi canción favorita.

    i. Miremos   9. la televisión.

    j. Habla   10. los deberes de química.

Translations:

Translate the following sentences into English:

1. Vayamos a la fiesta de fin de año.

_____

2. Deja tu bolso aquí.

_____

3. El jefe dijo, "Llegad temprano a trabajar el lunes."

_____

4. Mueve un pie después del otro.

_____

5. Pidamos ayuda a un experto en el tema.

_____

6. Escuche el sonido de los pájaros cantando.

_____

7. ¡Detened el coche inmediatamente!

_____

8. Deje de golpear la puerta.

_____

9. ¡Corramos fuera de la casa que se está quemando!

_____

10. Caminad muy lentamente y muy cuidadosamente.

_____

Story:

En un futuro no muy lejano, nuestro planeta Tierra podría ser totalmente diferente. Escuchad las **advertencias**, pues de eso puede depender el futuro de toda la humanidad. La tecnología avanza demasiado rápido. Después de tantos años de reírnos de la idea de robots **malvados** tomando control del planeta, ahora podría ser en serio. Día a día convivimos con inteligencia artificial en nuestros televisores, ordenadores y teléfonos móviles. Lo único que les falta son **cuerpos**, y podrían construirlos muy **fácilmente**. El mundo puede estar a punto de **cambiar**.

Imaginad un planeta **dominado** por robots. Un mundo donde un robot tenga el poder de decirnos "¡Camina! ¡Detente! ¡Ven para aquí! ¡Muévete hacia allá! ¡Trabaja! ¡No trabajes!" Ya no podremos tomar nuestras propias decisiones. ¿Y qué pasará si seguimos aprovechándonos del planeta **sin cuidado**? Pronto tendremos que usar **máscaras** que nos permitan **respirar**. ¡Ten cuidado! Porque ese podría ser el comienzo de nuestra transformación en androides: **mitad** robots y solo mitad humanos.

Vocabulary List:

1. advertencia - warning
2. malvados - evil
3. cuerpos - dodies
4. fácilmente - easily
5. cambiar - to change
6. dominado - dominated
7. sin cuidado - carelessly
8. máscaras - masks
9. respirar - to breathe
10. mitad - half

Translated Story:

In a future not very far away, our planet could be totally different. Listen to the **warnings** because the future of all of humanity could depend on it. Technology is moving forward too fast. After so many years of laughing at the idea of **evil** robots taking control of the planet, now it could be serious. Day by day, we live with artificial intelligence in our television, computers, and cellphones. The only thing they're missing is **bodies**, and they could build them very **easily**. Let's get ready! The world could be about to **change**.

Imagine a planet **dominated** by robots. A world where a robot has the power to tell us, "Walk! Stop! Come here! Move over there! Work! Don't work!" We won't be able to make our own decisions. And what will happen if we keep taking advantage of the world **carelessly**? Soon we will have to use **masks** that allow us to **breathe**. Be careful! Because that could be the beginning of our transformation into androids: half-robots and only **half-**human.

Questions:

1. ¿Cómo podrá ser el futuro en un futuro no muy lejano? _____

   How could the world be in a future not very far away?

2. ¿Qué debéis escuchar? _____

   What should be listened to?

3. ¿De qué idea nos reíamos? _____

   What idea did we used to laugh at?

4. ¿Qué le falta tener a la inteligencia artificial? _____

   What is artificial intelligence missing?

5. ¿Qué cosas podrían dominar el mundo? _____

   What things could dominate the world?

6. ¿Qué cosas nos pueden ayudar a respirar? _____

   What things could help us breathe?

Answers:

1.
      a. Abre

      b. Leamos

      c. Pinte

      d. Limpia

      e. Lavad

      f. Plantemos

      g. Dibuje

      h. Decide

      i. Partamos

      j. Doblad

2.
      a. ✗

      b. ✓

      c. ✓

      d. ✗

      e. ✓

      f. ✗

      g. ✗

      h. ✓

      i. ✓

      j. ✗

3.
      a. Tú

      b. Vosotros

      c. Usted

      d. Tú

      e. Vosotros

      f. Tú

g. Usted

h. Vosotros

i. Nosotros

j. Usted

4.

a. Sentar

b. Morir

c. Decir

d. Estar

e. Hacer

f. Dormir

g. Probar

h. Poner

i. Salir

j. Ser

5.

a. a-6: Camina un paso cada vez.

b. b-7: Vayamos juntos al cine.

c. c-8: Escuchad mi canción favorita.

d. d-1: Duerme temprano esta noche.

e. e-10: Hagamos los deberes de química.

f. f-4: Pida permiso antes de salir.

g. g-3: Bailad en la fiesta juntos.

h. h-2: Corre tan rápido como puedas.

i. i-9: Miremos la televisión.

j. j-5: Habla con tu mejor amigo.

Translations:

1. Let's go the end of the year party.

2. Leave your bag here.

3. The boss said, "Arrive early to work on Monday."

4. Move one foot after the other.

5. Let's ask for help from an expert on the subject.

6. Listen to the sound of the birds singing.

7. Stop the car immediately!

8. Stop knocking on the door.

9. Let's run out of the house that is burning!

10. Walk very slowly and very carefully.

Story:

1. Totalmente diferente.

2. Las advertencias.

3. Robots malvados.

4. Cuerpos.

5. Robots.

6. Máscaras.

Chapter 11
FUTURE WITH GOING TO

Pasado, presente y futuro. Past, present, and future. These are the main tenses used to talk in any language. They are a strict requirement to communicate in any language, and, of course, this includes Spanish. By now, you probably know the basics, but it is time to take a closer look at how to talk about the future in Spanish.

This is not the easiest subject, and there is more than one way to talk about the future in Spanish. In this lesson, we are going to focus on one particular way. This is the simplest and most used way to handle this, plus it is the most natural, so it fits in among native speakers.

In English, when you speak of something planned in the near future, you say "I'm going to the park tomorrow." In Spanish, this sentence would be "Voy al parque mañana." The way to form these sentences is as follows: **Personal pronoun + Ir ("to go") + Proposition a + Infinitive Verb.**

In Spanish, it is common to ignore the personal pronouns in these sentences to shorten them.

Negative sentences are exactly the same with a "No" in front of the "Ir a." And the questions are also the same sentences put between interrogation points "¿?"

Personal pronoun	Ir a
Yo	Voy a
Tú	Vas a
Él/Ella / Usted	Va a
Nosotros/as	Vamos a
Vosotros/as	Vais a
Ellos/as	Van a

Examples:

1. Voy a ir al cine el viernes.

   I'm going to go to the movie theater on Friday.

2. Él va a cocinar pizza esta noche.

   He is going to cook pizza tonight.

3. No vamos a conocer a la profesora.

   We are not going to meet the teacher.

4. ¿Vas a leer un libro nuevo?

   Are going to read a new book?

5. Virginia va a llamar a la policía.

   Virginia is going to call the police.

6. Vosotros vais a quedaros en un buen hotel.

   You are going to stay at a good hotel.

7. Ellos van a disfrutar el concierto.

   They are going to enjoy the concert.

Exercises:

1. Fill in the blanks with "Ir a" to match each personal pronoun in the following sentences:

    a. Yo _____ bañarme en la mañana.

    b. Nosotros _____ comprar un coche nuevo.

    c. Lucas _____ correr muy rápido.

    d. Tú _____ escribir un cuento.

    e. Mis hijas _____ hablar con el abuelo.

    f. El doctor no _____ trabajar esta semana.

    g. Yo no _____ ver la película de terror.

    h. Vosotros _____ pedir ayudar profesional.

    i. Ella no _____ nadar en la playa.

    j. Usted _____ beber vino blanco.

2. Transform these sentences from present to future tense:

    a. Yo visito el museo.

    _____

    b. Tú no plantas un árbol.

    _____

    c. Vosotros bailáis en la fiesta.

    _____

    d. Mi tío cocina mucha comida.

    _____

    e. Ella pinta la pared.

    _____

    f. Nosotros escuchamos las noticias.

    _____

    g. Él conduce el coche.

    _____

    h. Usted duerme toda la noche.

    _____

    i. Yo vendo ropa usada.

    _____

j.   Vosotros tomáis buenas decisiones.

_____

3. Translate the verb to complete the sentences:

   a. Usted va a (drink) _____ agua fría.

   b. Ricardo va a (read) _____ el periódico.

   c. Nosotros vamos a (play) _____ un juego.

   d. Yo no voy a (call) _____ a mi madre.

   e. Tú vas a (open) _____ la puerta.

   f. Pedro va a (travel) _____ a Rusia.

   g. Ellos van a (study) _____toda la tarde.

   h. Mis amigas no van a (jump) _____ la cuerda.

   i. Nosotros vamos a (observe) _____ los animales.

   j. Yo voy a (close) _____ la ventana.

4. Translate the following sentences from English to Spanish:

   a. I am going to cry.

_____

   b. They are going to clean.

_____

   c. You are going to eat.

_____

   d. We are going to swim.

_____

   e. Jack is going to draw.

_____

   f. I am not going to sleep.

_____

   g. The boys are going to run.

_____

   h. Lucy is going to travel.

_____

   i. You are not going to cook.

j.   We are going to scream.

5.   Put the words in order to form sentences that make sense:

a.   usted - cocinar - a - pasta - va

b.   en - nosotros - avión - viajar - vamos - a

c.   tú - la - a - puerta - golpear - vas

d.   caer - el - a - se - va - árbol

e.   a - vosotros - llorar - vais

f.   coche - a - tú - conducir - vas - un

g.   la - cena - a - cocinar - va

h.   vas - guitarra - tocar - a

i.   el - voy - lavar - a - coche

j.   la - vamos - apagar - a - luz

Translations:

Translate the following sentences into English:

1. Vamos a ir juntos a la playa este año.

_____

2. Javier va a estudiar medicina en la universidad.

_____

3. No vas a llegar a tiempo al trabajo hoy.

_____

4. Vais a construir una casa en el árbol.

_____

5. ¿Vas a ir conmigo a la fiesta de cumpleaños?

_____

6. No voy a adoptar otro gato.

_____

7. ¿Vamos a ir a clases mañana?

_____

8. Usted va a arrepentirse de decir estas palabras.

_____

9. Rosa va a cantar mi canción favorita en el concierto.

_____

10. Nosotros vamos a comprar regalos de navidad hoy.

_____

Story:

Se acerca el fin de las clases en el colegio. Es un colegio **privado**, y muy **prestigioso**. Los estudiantes de este colegio son muy **competitivos**: todos quieren ser los **mejores**, y aprovechan cualquier oportunidad para **demostrar** que son los mejores. En este caso, se trata de los proyectos de fin de año. Antes de que terminen las clases, los estudiantes van a preparar una presentación especial. Las presentaciones van a ser sobre algo que los niños aprendieron ese año.

Los estudiantes se tomaron estos proyectos como una **competencia**. Eso significa que todos van a **intentar** hacer algo mejor que los demás. Un grupo de amigas va a hacer un baile sobre distintas épocas de la historia. Andrés va a pintar un mural sobre el arte en las civilizaciones **antiguas**. Carmen va a cocinar platos de comida de todo el mundo. Pero parece que el **ganador** va a ser Miguel. Este niño va a hacer un **discurso** sobre sus mejores amigos, sobre los cuales aprendió mucho este año.

Vocabulary List:

1. privado - private
2. prestigioso - prestigious
3. competitivos - competitive
4. mejores - best
5. demostrar - to prove

6. competencia - competition
7. intentar - to try
8. antiguas - ancient
9. ganador - winner
10. discurso - speech

Translated Story:

The end-of-school classes are drawing near. It is a **private** school and very **prestigious**. The students at this school are very **competitive**; they all want to be the **best**. And they take every opportunity to **prove** that they are the best. In this case, it is the year-end projects. Before classes end, the students will prepare a special presentation. The presentations will be about something the children learned that year.

The students took on these projects as a **competition**. That means everyone is going to **try** to do something better than everyone else. A group of friends is going to do a dance about different periods of history. Andrés is going to paint a mural about art in **ancient** civilizations. Carmen is going to cook food dishes from all over the world. But it seems that the **winner** is going to be Miguel. This boy is going to make a **speech** about his best friends, who he learned a lot about this year.

Questions:

1. ¿Qué está acercándose? _____

   What is drawing near?

2. ¿Cómo es el colegio? _____

   What is the school like?

3. ¿Cómo son los estudiantes? _____

   How are the students?

4. ¿Qué van a preparar los estudiantes? _____

   What are the students going to prepare?

5. ¿Sobre qué es el mural? _____

   What is the mural about?

6. ¿Qué va a hacer Miguel? _____

   What is Miguel going to do?

Answers:

1.

    a. voy a

    b. vamos a

    c. va a

    d. vas a

    e. van a

    f. va a

    g. voy a

    h. van a

    i. va a

    j. va a

2.

    a. Yo voy a visitar el museo.

    b. Tú no vas a plantar un árbol.

    c. Vosotros vais a bailar en la fiesta.

    d. Mi tío va a cocinar mucha comida.

    e. Ella va a pintar la pared.

    f. Nosotros vamos a escuchar las noticias.

    g. Él va a conducir el coche.

    h. Usted va a dormir toda la noche.

    i. Yo voy a vender ropa usada.

    j. Vosotros vais a tomar buenas decisiones.

3.

    a. tomar/beber

    b. leer

    c. jugar

    d. llamar

    e. abrir

    f. viajar

g. estudiar

h. saltar

i. observar

j. cerrar

4.

    a. Yo voy a llorar.

    b. Ellos van a limpiar.

    c. Tú vas a comer.

    d. Nosotros vamos a nadar.

    e. Jack va a dibujar.

    f. Yo no voy a dormir.

    g. Los niños van a correr.

    h. Lucy va a viajar.

    i. Tú no vas a cocinar.

    j. Nosotros vamos a gritar.

5.

    a. Usted va a cocinar pasta.

    b. Nosotros vamos a viajar en avión.

    c. Tú vas a golpear la puerta.

    d. El árbol se va a caer.

    e. Vosotros vais a llorar.

    f. Tú vas a conducir un coche.

    g. Va a cocinar la cena.

    h. Vas a tocar guitarra.

    i. Voy a lavar el coche.

    j. Vamos a apagar la luz.

Translations:

1. We are going to go to the beach together this year.

2. Javier is going to study medicine at university.

3. You are not going to arrive on time at work today.

4. They are going to build a treehouse.

5. Are you going to go to the birthday party with me?

6. I am not going to adopt another cat.

7. Are we going to go to classes tomorrow?

8. You are going to regret saying these words.

9. Rosa is going to sing my favorite song in the concert.

10. We are going to buy Christmas presents today.

Story:

1. El fin de las clases en el colegio.

2. Privado y muy prestigioso.

3. Muy competitivos.

4. Presentaciones especiales.

5. El arte en las civilizaciones antiguas.

6. Hacer un discurso sobre sus mejores amigos.

Chapter 12
SER, ESTAR, TENER, OR HABER?

A very important part of becoming a fluent Spanish speaker is to handle the most common verbs in this language. We are talking about *"ser, estar, tener,* and *haber."* They can be a little tricky, and beginners may get confused at first, but with this guide and enough practice, they won't be a problem at all. It's only a matter of taking a close look at each of them.

Ser: To be (state of being)

The verb *Ser* is used to state a fact about a person. For example, You are tall. He is Canadian. They are kind.

In Spanish, the verb *Ser* is conjugated this way:

Ser			
Person	**Past**	**Present**	**Future**
Yo	Fui	Soy	Seré
Tú	Fuiste	Eres	Serás
Él/Ella Usted	Fue	Es	Será
Nosotros/as	Fuimos	Somos	Seremos
Vosotros/as	Fuisteis	Sois	Seréis
Ellos/as	Fueron	Son	Serán

Examples:

1. Yo soy profesora de matemáticas.

   I am a math teacher.

2. Tú fuiste mi mejor amiga.

   You were my best friend.

3. Usted será el jefe de la compañía.

   You will be the boss of the company.

   Estar: To be (temporary condition)

   Meanwhile, the verb *Estar* is more precise and limited. It is used to describe a temporary characteristic or condition - something that isn't necessarily permanent. In English, it's the same verb - *to be*. For example: I am scared. We are on vacation. They are mad at each other. In Spanish, it's a little different, as we're about to see.

Estar			
Person	**Past**	**Present**	**Future**
Yo	Estuve	Estoy	Estaré
Tú	Estuviste	Estás	Estarás
Él/EllaUsted	Estuvo	Está	Estará
Nosotros/as	Estuvimos	Estamos	Estaremos
Vosotros/as	Estuvisteis	Estáis	Estaréis
Ellos/as	Estuvieron	Están	Estarán

Examples:

1. Tú estás trabajando en la oficina.
   You are working at the office.

2. Nosotros estaremos en la fiesta este viernes.
   We will be at the party this Friday.

3. Sofía estuvo enferma la semana pasada.
   Sofía was sick last week.

Tener: To have (to own, have to, must, obligation)

The verb *Tener* is a very interesting one in English and Spanish. *Have* can express ownership of something, e.g., I have a red car. *Have to* is used to express an obligation: I have to go to school. This can be applied in Spanish as well when adding the word que to the verb - *Tener que*.

Tener			
Person	**Past**	**Present**	**Future**
Yo	Tuve	Tengo	Tendré
Tú	Tuviste	Tienes	Tendrás
Él/Ella/ Usted	Tuvo	Tiene	Tendrá
Nosotros/as	Tuvimos	Tenemos	Tendremos
Vosotros/as	Tuvisteis	Tenéis	Tendréis
/Ellos/as	Tuvieron	Tienen	Tendrán

Examples:

1. Vosotros tenéis que ir a esta reunión.
   You have to go to this meeting.

2. Gregorio tuvo que vender su casa.
   Gregorio had to sell his house.

3. Tú tendrás que buscar un abogado.
   You will have to look for a lawyer.

4. Yo no tengo mucho tiempo esta mañana.
   I don't have much time this morning.

Haber: To have / have to (there was, there is, there will be)

Last, but not least, is the verb *Haber*, which has a very particular use in Spanish. It is only conjugated in the 3rd person singular:

- Past: Hubo
- Present: Hay
- Future: Habrá

It is used to state a fact or a responsibility. For example, in English, when we say, "There's a hole in the wall," or "One has to be careful here," in Spanish, it would be, "Hay un hoyo en la pared," or "Hay que ser cuidadoso aquí."

Examples:

1. Hubo un problema en la oficina esta mañana.
   There was a problem at the office this morning.

2. Hay que lavarse las manos con agua y jabón.
   One has to wash one's hands with water and soap.

3. Habrá un concierto de jazz en junio.
   There will be a jazz concert in June.

Now that you know the basics of these very important verbs in Spanish, you'll notice they are the most used in this language. This will be a very important lesson in your journey, so make sure to go through it as many times as you need. *¡Hay que estudiar mucho!*

Examples:

1. Yo soy profesor de matemáticas.
   I am a math teacher.

2. Ellas estuvieron enfermas ayer.
   They were sick yesterday.

3. Tú tendrás un gran regalo.

   You will have a great gift.

4. Hay una mancha en la camisa.

   There is a stain on the shirt.

5. Nosotros estamos en las montañas.

   We are in the mountains.

Exercises:

1. Connect the Spanish sentences with the English translation:

   a. Yo tengo un resfriado.   1. My mom was sad.

   b. Ella fue feliz.   2. Pedro will be a lawyer.

   c. Hay mucha comida.   3. She was happy.

   d. Nosotros estamos aquí.   4. There will be little snow.

   e. Mi madre estuvo triste.   5. You were afraid.

   f. Los niños están dormidos.   6. There is a lot of food.

   g. Pedro será abogado.   7. Fernanda will have homework.

   h. Tú tuviste miedo.   8. We are here.

   i. Fernanda tendrá deberes.   9. The children are asleep.

   j. Habrá poca nieve.   10. I have a cold.

2. Complete the sentences using "ser, estar, tener, or haber." Conjugate as necessary in the present tense:

   a. Nosotros _____ en México.

   b. Teresa _____ doctora.

   c. _____ muchos coches en la calle.

   d. Yo _____ que irme a casa.

   e. Ellas _____ mejores amigas.

   f. Tú _____ que dormir esta noche.

   g. _____ cuatro ventanas en la casa.

   h. Esteban _____ colombiano.

   i. Yo _____ dolor de cabeza.

   j. Usted _____ en el hospital.

3. Write the English equivalent of the following Spanish sentences:

   a. Yo soy   _____

   b. Usted tiene   _____

   c. Hannah fue   _____

   d. Tú serás   _____

   e. Nosotros estuvimos   _____

f. Yo tendré _____

g. Nicolás es _____

h. Ellos tendrán _____

i. Ellas fueron _____

j. Tú estás _____

4. Write the Spanish conjugation according to the instructions:

a. Tú + ser + present tense _____

b. Nosotros + estar + past tense _____

c. Amanda + tener + present tense _____

d. Vosotros + estar + future tense _____

e. Yo + tener + past tense _____

f. Ellos + ser + future tense _____

g. Felipe + estar + present tense _____

h. Usted + ser + future tense _____

i. Yo + estar + past tense _____

j. Nosotros + tener + present tense _____

5. Circle the correct word from the parenthesis to match the rest of the sentence:

a. Vosotros (ser/tenéis) mucha hambre.

b. Yo (fui/hay) estudiante de medicina.

c. (Hay/Estar) un león en el zoológico.

d. Él (serán /será) mi novio.

e. Tú (tendrás /estarás) dormida en la noche.

f. Nosotros (fuimos/estuvimos) ganadores.

g. (Ser/Habrá) una reunión aquí.

h. Usted (fue/estuvo) en el ejército.

i. Ellos (tendrán/serán) poco tiempo libre.

j. Yo (tuve/soy) una mujer americana.

Translations:

Translate the following sentences into English:

1. Hay muchos problemas en este país.

_____

2. Yo seré una excelente hermana mayor.

_____

3. Camila tendrá que trabajar muy duro este mes.

_____

4. Ellos estaban en problemas, pero encontraron la solución.

_____

5. Nosotros estaremos en Canadá en julio.

_____

6. Hubo solo veinte personas en la fiesta del sábado.

_____

7. Gerardo tuvo que cocinar toda la tarde.

_____

8. Mi mejor amiga fue la mejor de la clase.

_____

9. Todos los niños estarán jugando en el parque.

_____

10. Esta película es mi favorita de todos los tiempos.

_____

Story:

A los siete años de edad, lo más importante para los niños es **divertirse**. En el colegio, lo que más les interesa a los niños es pasarlo bien y hacer buenos amigos. La mayor parte del tiempo, los niños se entretienen jugando. Cuando hablan entre ellos, hablan de series de televisión, superhéroes, y sus **juegos** favoritos. Así que, cuando llegó el día de presentar a sus **padres** frente a la clase, todos los niños se sorprendieron mucho al aprender sobre las familias de sus amigos.

El padre de Alejandro dijo,:"Yo fui doctor en el hospital de la ciudad. Yo estuve presente cuando muchos de ustedes **nacieron**." La madre de Mariana dijo: "Yo soy parte del **ejército**. No os puedo decir mucho más. Yo tengo que **mantener** muchos secretos." La madre de Verónica dijo: "Yo soy veterinaria, y estoy trabajando en el **refugio** de animales. Hay muchos animales que necesitan amor. ¿Quién quiere ir a **visitarlo**?"

Todos los niños fueron muy felices. Aprendieron mucho, se divirtieron, y ahora están **invitados** a visitar el refugio de animales. Seguramente más de uno será el nuevo **dueño** del perro o gato que adoptará.

Vocabulary List:

1. divertirse - to have fun
2. juegos - games
3. padres - parents
4. nacieron - were born
5. ejército - army
6. mantener - to keep
7. refugio – shelter
8. visitar - to visit
9. invitados - invited
10. dueño - owner

Translated Story:

At seven years of age, the most important thing for children is to have fun. At school, what matters most to children is **having fun** and making good friends. Most of the time, the children entertain themselves by playing. When they talk to each other, they talk about TV shows, superheroes, and their favorite **games**. So when the day came to introduce their **parents** in front of the class, all the children were very surprised to learn about their friends' families.

Alejandro's father said, "I was a doctor at the city hospital. I was present when many of you were **born**." Mariana's mom said, "I'm part of the **army**. I can't tell you much more. I have to **keep** a lot of secrets." Veronica's mom said, "I'm a veterinarian, and I'm working at the animal **shelter**. There are many animals that need love. Who wants to go to **visit**?"

All the children were very happy. They learned a lot, had fun, and are now **invited** to visit the animal shelter. Surely more than one will be the new **owner** of the dog or cat that they will adopt.

Questions:

1. ¿Qué es lo más importante para los niños? _____

   What is the most important thing for 7-year-olds?

2. ¿Sobre qué hablan los niños? _____

   What do kids talk about?

3. ¿Dónde tenían que presentar a los padres? _____

   Where did they have to introduce their parents?

4. ¿El padre de quién era un doctor? _____

   Whose father was a doctor?

5. ¿Dónde trabaja la veterinaria? _____

   Where does the veterinarian work?

6. ¿Qué necesitan los animales? _____

   What do animals need?

Answers:

1.

    a. a-10

    b. b-3

    c. c-6

    d. d-8

    e. e-1

    f. f-9

    g. g-2

    h. h-5

    i. i-7

    j. j-4

2.

    a. estamos

    b. es

    c. hay

    d. tengo

    e. son

    f. tienes

    g. hay

    h. es

    i. tengo

    j. está

3.

    a. I am

    b. You have

    c. Hannah was

    d. You will be

    e. We were

    f. I will have

g. Nicolás is

h. They will have

i. They were

j. You are

4.

a. eres

b. estuvimos

c. tiene

d. estaréis

e. tuve

f. serán

g. está

h. será

i. estuve

j. tenemos

5.

a. tenéis

b. fui

c. hay

d. será

e. estarás

f. fuimos

g. habrá

h. estuvo

i. tendrán

j. soy

Translations:

1. There are many problems in this country.
2. I will be an excellent older sister.
3. Camila will have to work very hard this month.
4. They were in trouble, but found the solution.
5. We will be in Canada in July.
6. There were only twenty people at the party on Saturday.
7. Gerardo had to cook all afternoon.
8. My best friend was the best in the class.
9. All the children will be playing in the park.
10. This movie is my favorite of all time.

Story:

1. Divertirse.
2. Series de televisión, superhéroes, y sus juegos favoritos.
3. Frente a la clase.
4. El padre de Alejandro.
5. En el refugio de animales.
6. Amor.

Chapter 13
COMPARATIVES AND SUPERLATIVES

When learning Spanish, you will find yourself needing to describe many subjects, like people, places, and everyday things. Usually, when describing something, we tend to compare it to something else as a reference. In English, we might say this person is taller than that person, this house is better than that house, this is the best pizza in the city. These are what are known as comparatives and superlatives.

It is time to learn how to use comparatives and superlatives properly in Spanish. Let's start with **comparatives**. This is the basic formula to form the main two comparative types of sentences:

- **More than**: A + *ser* (soy, eres, es, somos, sois, son) + **más** + adjective + que + B
- **Less than:** A + *ser* (soy, eres, es, somos, sois, son) + **menos** + adjective + que + B

Examples:

1. Yo soy más joven que tú.
   I am younger than you.

2. Luis es menos fuerte que Javier.
   Luis is less strong than Javier.

3. Nosotros somos más rápidos que vosotros.
   We are faster than you.

Next, we will review **superlatives**.

- **The most**: A + *ser* (soy, eres, es, somos, sois, son) + el/la/los/las}+ noun + **más** + adjective (+ de/del + location)
- **The least:** A + *ser* (soy, eres, es, somos, sois, son) + el/la/los/las}+ noun + **menos** + adjective (+ de/del + location)
Examples:

1. Tú eres la niña más bonita.

   You are the prettiest girl.

2. Este es el coche más rápido del mundo.

   This is the fastest car in the world

3. Julio es el mes menos frío.

   July is the least cold month.

Lastly, we must take a look at **irregular** comparatives and superlatives. In English, we know them as "better, the best, worse, the worst," and more. In Spanish, we say that something can be "**mejor que**" (better than) something else or that it can be "**el mejor**" (the best) out of all the others.

This means that instead of using "**más** + adjective" or "**menos** + adjective," you will use a word from the following list for comparatives, and add "el/la/los/las" + one of the words of the list for superlatives.

Remember to notice if the subject is singular or plural, so that the comparatives and superlatives match. In case of a plural subject, you'll need to add "-es" at the end.

- Good → bueno → Best/better → mejor

    - Ella es la mejor jugadora de tenis. - She is the best tennis player.

    - Nosotros somos mejores cocineros que ellos. - We are better cooks than them.

- Bad → malo → Worse → peor

    - Este trabajo es peor que el anterior. - This job is worse than the previous one.

    - Esta es la peor parte de la ciudad. - This is the worst part of the city.

- Big/old → grande/viejo → Biggest/oldest → mayor

    - Juliana es la hermana mayor de Edgar. - Juliana is Edgar's oldest sister.

    - Mi casa es de mayor tamaño que un apartamento. – My house is a bigger size than an apartment.

- Small/young → pequeño/joven → Smallest/youngest → menor

  ○ Tú eres la menor de tus hermanas. - You are the youngest of your sisters.

  ○ Andreina es menor que mi prima. - Andreina is younger than my cousin.

Note: In Spanish, it is wrong to say the following things: "El más/menos mejor/bueno" or "El más/menos malo/peor." You can only say "el mejor" or "el peor."

Examples:

1. Ella es la mejor pianista.
   She is the best pianist.

2. Manuel es el mayor de la familia.
   Manuel is the oldest of the family.

3. Este es el menor de los problemas.
   This is the smallest of the problems.

Exercises:

1. Read and understand these Spanish sentences, then match them with the correct half in the other column:

   a. 8 am es más temprano que   1. un enano.

   b. Un gigante es más alto que   2. mi hijo.

   c. La tortuga no es más rápida que   3. un ratón.

   d. La oficina es más grande que   4. el baño.

   e. El sol es más caliente que   5. el verano.

   f. La noche es más tarde que   6. un zapato.

   g. Mi abuelo es mayor que   7. la mañana.

   h. Un oso es más pesado que   8. 10 am.

   i. El invierno es más frío que   9. la luna.

   j. Un diamante es más caro que   10. la liebre.

2. Organize the words in the correct order to form sentences:

   a. yo - pequeña - más - soy

   _____

   b. caliente - menos - la - está - sopa

   _____

   c. más - caminar - lento - es

   _____

   d. tú - bailarina - mejor - eres - la

   _____

   e. azul - menos - el - no - cielo - es

   _____

   f. canción - la - peor

   _____

   g. no - es - más - el - trabajo - fácil

   _____

   h. la - Judith - doctora - mejor - es

   _____

   i. más - la - temprano - fiesta - es

168

j. es - casa - la - limpia - menos - esta

3. Write these English comparative adjectives in Spanish as "más + adjective":

   a. Happier _____

   b. Smarter _____

   c. Slower _____

   d. Prettier _____

   e. Scarier _____

   f. Longer _____

   g. Colder _____

   h. Sadder _____

   i. Cheaper _____

   j. Taller _____

4. Write these English superlatives in Spanish as "el más + adjective":

   a. Fastest _____

   b. Shortest _____

   c. Loudest _____

   d. Messiest _____

   e. Shiest _____

   f. Laziest _____

   g. Sweetest _____

   h. Hottest _____

   i. Easiest _____

   j. Cleanest _____

5. Translate the following superlatives to English:

   a. El mejor cantante. _____

   b. El animal más grande. _____

   c. La hija menor. _____

   d. El peor juego. _____

e. El libro más largo. _____

f. Las estrellas más brillantes. _____

g. Las comidas menos dulces. _____

h. El hombre menos divertido. _____

i. La mejor clase. _____

j. Los árboles más verdes. _____

Translations:

Translate the following sentences into English:

1. Maribel es la mejor profesora de la escuela.

_____

2. Este año tuve el mejor pastel de cumpleaños de toda mi vida.

_____

3. Mi gato no es más joven que mi perro.

_____

4. Mi trabajo es más largo que tu trabajo, pero no es más difícil.

_____

5. El miércoles no es peor que el lunes.

_____

6. Jenny es más alta que su hijo.

_____

7. Mi tío es mejor cocinero que mi tía.

_____

8. Victoria es la mejor fotógrafa de la ciudad.

_____

9. Este es el día más largo de toda mi vida.

_____

10. Mercy tiene la peor personalidad de mi familia.

_____

Story:

Es natural, en todas las familias, que los hermanos sean **competitivos**. Se dice que incluso desde el **vientre** de la madre, los gemelos empiezan a **pelear** entre sí. Cuando son bebés, un hermano quiere tener más y mejores **juguetes** que el resto. Cuando van al colegio, un hermano quiere tener mejores **notas** y más amigos que los demás. Cuando son adultos, un hermano quiere tener el mejor trabajo y la casa más grande que los otros. Sin embargo, algunas familias llevan la competencia al extremo. Este es el caso de la familia Ávila, con cuatro hermanos que, sobre todo, compiten: Andrés, Esteban, Ricardo y Paul.

Los hermanos nacieron con solo un año de diferencia entre cada uno, así que crecieron más o menos al mismo **ritmo**. Andrés aprendió a **leer** más rápido que Esteban, pero Ricardo es mejor escritor que sus hermanos. Paul es el hermano que sufrió menos **enfermedades**, pero Esteban es el hermano más fuerte de todos. Andrés tiene la **novia** más bonita, y Paul tiene el mejor coche. Esteban es más alto que Paul, y Ricardo es mejor cantante que Andrés. Ricardo se graduó más temprano que Paul, y Esteban es mejor **cocinero** que Andrés. Los cuatro hermanos compiten por cada parte de sus vidas, pero aun así, sus padres siempre han dicho que a los cuatro hermanos los quieren por igual.

Vocabulary List:

1. competitivos – competitive
2. vientre - womb
3. pelear - to fight
4. juguetes - toys
5. notas - grades
6. ritmo - rhythm
7. leer - to read
8. enfermedades - illnesses
9. novia - girlfriend
10. cocinero - cook

Translated Story:

It's natural, in all families, that siblings are **competitive**. It's said that even from the **womb** of the mother, twins start to **fight** with each other. When they are babies, one sibling wants to have more and better **toys** than the rest. When they go to school, one sibling wants to have better **grades** and more friends than the others. When they are adults, one sibling wants to have the best job and the biggest house than the others. However, some families take the competition to the extreme. This is the case of the Avila family with four siblings who compete about everything: Andrés, Esteban, Ricardo, and Paul.

The siblings were born with just one year of difference between each of them, so they grew up more or less at the same **rhythm**. Andres learned to **read** faster than Esteban, but Ricardo is a better writer than his siblings. Paul is the brother that least suffered **illnesses**, but Esteban is the strongest brother of all. Andres has the prettiest **girlfriend**, and Paul has the best car. Esteban is taller than Paul, and Ricardo is a better singer than Andrés. Ricardo graduated earlier than Paul, and Esteban is a better **cook** than Andrés. The four brothers compete in every part of their lives, but even so, their parents have always said that they love the four brothers the same.

Questions:

1. ¿Dónde empiezan a pelearse los gemelos? _____

   Where do twins start fighting?

2. ¿Qué quieren tener los bebés? _____

   What do babies want to have?

3. ¿Cuándo quieren tener el mejor trabajo y la casa más grande? _____

   _____

   When do they want to have the best job and the biggest house?

4. ¿Cuántos hermanos hay en la familia Ávila? _____

   ¿How many siblings are in the Ávila family?

5. ¿Cuántos años de diferencia hay entre cada uno de los hermanos? _____

   _____

   How many years of difference are between each of the brothers?

6. ¿Quién es el mejor escritor? _____

   Who is the best writer?

Answers:

1.

     a. 10 am

     b. Un enano

     c. La liebre

     d. El baño

     e. La luna

     f. La mañana

     g. Mi hijo

     h. Un ratón

     i. El verano

     j. Un zapato

2.

     a. Yo soy más pequeña.

     b. La sopa está menos caliente.

     c. Caminar es más lento.

     d. Tú eres la mejor bailarina.

     e. El cielo no es menos azul.

     f. La peor canción.

     g. No es el trabajo más fácil.

     h. Judith es la mejor doctora.

     i. La fiesta es más temprano.

     j. Esta es la casa menos limpia.

3.

     a. Más feliz

     b. Más inteligente

     c. Más lento

     d. Más bonito

     e. Más aterrador

     f. Más largo

    g. Más frío

    h. Más triste

    i. Más barato

    j. Más alto

4.

    a. El más rápido

    b. El más corto

    c. El más ruidoso

    d. El más desordenado

    e. El más tímido

    f. El más perezoso

    g. El más dulce

    h. El más caliente

    i. El más fácil

    j. El más limpio

5.

    a. The best singer.

    b. The biggest animal.

    c. The youngest daughter.

    d. The worst game.

    e. The longest book.

    f. The brightest stars.

    g. The least sweet foods.

    h. The least funny man.

    i. The best class.

    j. The greenest trees.

Translations:

1. Maribel is the best teacher in the school.

2. This year I had the best birthday cake of all my life.

3. My cat is not younger than my dog.

4. My work is longer than your work, but it isn't more difficult.

5. Wednesday is not worse than Monday.

6. Jenny is taller than her son.

7. My uncle is a better cook than my aunt.

8. Victoria is the best photographer in the city.

9. This is the longest day of my life.

10. Mercy has the worst personality in my family.

Story:

1. Desde el vientre de la madre.

2. Más y mejores juguetes.

3. Cuando son adultos.

4. Cuatro hermanos.

5. Un año.

6. Ricardo.

Chapter 14
PRESENT CONTINUOUS

The present continuous is a very important part of communicating in a language. It might feel like it comes very naturally, as we talk mostly about the present in day-to-day conversations. However, there are certain things that are extremely important to understand about the present continuous when we are learning Spanish.

In Spanish, present continuous is *strictly* used when talking about things that are currently happening at the exact moment we are speaking, no other time. In English, we might say "I am walking to the park tomorrow," but in Spanish, that wouldn't make sense. You can only say "Yo estoy caminando hacia el parque" while you are in the process of performing the action.

To form present continuous sentences, you need a very simple formula: **subject + verb to be + gerund of a verb**. In Spanish, this would be: **sujeto + present tense of the verb "estar" + gerund of a verb.**

We have seen the present tense of the verb "*estar*" before:

- I am - Yo estoy
- You are - Tú estás
- He/She/It is - Él/Ella/Eso/Usted está
- We are - Nosotros estamos
- You are – Vosotros estáis
- They are - Ellos/Ellas están

The gerund of a verb depends on a case-by-case basis.

Verbs ending in **-ar** change to **-ando**:

- To walk: Caminar - Caminando
- To sing: Cantar - Cantando
- To study: Estudiar - Estudiando

Verbs ending in **-ir** or **-er** change to **-iendo**:

- To write: Escribir - Escribiendo

- To eat: Comer - Comiendo
- To do: Hacer - Haciendo

Lastly, there are some irregular verbs that change more of their form.

- To read: Leer - Leyendo
- To see: Ver - Viendo
- To sleep: Dormir - Durmiendo
- To say: Decir - Diciendo
- To ask: Pedir - Pidiendo
- To go: Ir - Yendo
- To listen: Oír - Oyendo

Examples:

1. Mi padre está cantando mi canción favorita.

   My dad is singing my favorite song.

2. Fabiana está pintando la pared.

   Fabiana is painting the wall.

3. Ella está escribiendo una carta.

   She is writing a letter.

4. Ellos están viviendo en mi casa.

   They are living in my house.

5. El gato está durmiendo en la cocina.

   The cat is sleeping in the kitchen.

Exercises:

1. Transform these sentences from present simple to present continuous:

    a. Yo camino rápido.   _____

    b. Tú estudias francés.   _____

    c. Él salta alto.   _____

    d. Ella toca la guitarra.   _____

    e. Usted limpia el piso.   _____

    f. Nosotros cantamos juntos.   _____

    g. Vosotros veis la película.   _____

    h. Ellos escuchan la radio.   _____

    i. Ellas nadan en la playa.   _____

    j. Yo rompo un papel.   _____

2. Complete these sentences writing the gerund of the verb in parenthesis:

    a. Valeria está (aprender) _____ a cocinar.

    b. Usted está (conducir) _____ un coche.

    c. Nosotros estamos (ir) _____ al teatro.

    d. Yo estoy (pintar) _____ un cuadro.

    e. Él está (hacer) _____ una foto.

    f. Ellas están (construir) _____ una casa.

    g. Tú estás (bañar) _____ al perro.

    h. El niño está (decir) _____ mentiras.

    i. Ella está (doblar) _____ una hoja.

    j. El agua está (hervir) _____ en la cocina.

3. Translate these gerunds of verbs in English to Spanish:

    a. Walking   _____

    b. Reading   _____

    c. Cutting   _____

    d. Fighting   _____

    e. Hitting   _____

    f. Playing   _____

g. Touching   _____

h. Moving   _____

i. Breaking   _____

j. Traveling   _____

4. Write ✓ if the sentence is written correctly or ✗ if it isn't:

     a. Nosotros somos caminando hoy.   _____

     b. Tú estás ver la televisión.   _____

     c. Ellos están comiendo helados.   _____

     d. Enrique va a escribiendo una carta.   _____

     e. Mi padre está lavando el coche.   _____

     f. Yo estuve nadar en la piscina.   _____

     g. Luisa está viendo una película.   _____

     h. Usted está conduciendo un camión.   _____

     i. María es volar como un ave.   _____

     j. Vosotros sois peleando mucho.   _____

5. Choose the right verb that fits with the rest of the sentence:

     a. Ángel está bebiendo/durmiendo vino.

     b. Emma está escribiendo/muriendo una carta.

     c. Los niños están trabajando/escuchando a la madre.

     d. Yo estoy caminando/nadando por el museo.

     e. El pájaro está peleando/volando en el cielo.

     f. Ellos están viendo/comiendo el postre.

     g. Mi novia está viajando/oyendo por Europa.

     h. Tú estás cocinando/golpeando la cena.

     i. Ella está jugando/leyendo un libro.

     j. Nosotros estamos estudiando/construyendo historia.

Translations:

Translate the following sentences into English:

1. Mi madre está arreglando el jardín de la casa.

_____

2. El estudiante está leyendo un libro nuevo.

_____

3. Tú estás bailando muy bien.

_____

4. Nosotros estamos trabajando juntos en este proyecto.

_____

5. Usted está comiendo una ensalada.

_____

6. Yo estoy hablando con una compañera de trabajo.

_____

7. Él está muriendo de sed.

_____

8. No me estás oyendo mientras estoy hablando.

_____

9. El perro está corriendo de un lado a otro.

_____

10. Mis hermanos están bebiendo para celebrar.

_____

Story:

Cuando Harry se **mudó** a Europa, el primer año fue muy difícil. "**Por fin** estoy viviendo en Europa" se dijo Harry a sí mismo. "¿Qué tan difícil podría ser?" se preguntó. Pronto, Harry descubrió que sería muy difícil. Todo empezó en España. "Aquí todos están hablando español, igual que yo. **Seguramente** será muy fácil hacer amigos" pensó Harry. Al poco tiempo se dio cuenta de que se equivocó. Los españoles eran todos muy diferentes, y tuvo la mala **suerte** de encontrarse solo con personas que no lo aceptaban. Pero Harry no se rindió, y volvió a intentar empezar de nuevo.

"Muy bien, ahora estoy viviendo en Finlandia. Estoy caminando sobre la **nieve** y estoy usando grandes **abrigos**. Esto va a ser divertido" pensó Harry cuando se mudó a Finlandia. Pero, aunque las personas fueron muy **amables**, no logró **acostumbrarse** al clima, y tuvo que irse de nuevo.

"Ahora estoy viviendo en Bélgica, pero ¡no logro entender los idiomas!" se **quejó** Harry. "Quizá no hay lugar como el hogar… a menos que ¿quizá la mejor parte de este año fue viajar tanto?" se preguntó Harry. Y así fue como este **viajero** decidió explorar toda Europa, acumular nuevos amigos, y aprender muchos idiomas, hasta encontrar su verdadero hogar.

Vocabulary List:

1. mudo – moved
2. por fin - finally
3. seguramente - surely
4. suerte - luck
5. nieve - snow
6. abrigos - coats
7. amables - kind
8. acostumbrarse - to get used to
9. quejó - complained
10. viajero - traveler

Translated Story:

When Harry **moved** to Europe, the first year was very difficult. "I'm **finally** living in Europe," Harry told himself. "How difficult could it be?" he asked himself. Soon, Harry discovered that it would be very difficult. It all started in Spain. "Everyone here is speaking Spanish, just like me. **Surely,** it'll be easy to make friends," Harry thought. Before long, he realized that he was wrong. The Spanish were all very different, and he had the bad **luck** of finding himself alone with people who did not accept him. But Harry didn't give up, and he tried to start over again.

"Very well, now I am living in Finland. I'm walking in the **snow,** and I'm wearing big **coats.** This is going to be fun," Harry thought when he moved to Finland. But, although the people were very **kind**, he couldn't **get used to** the weather, and he had to leave again.

"Now I am living in Belgium, but I can't manage to understand the languages!" Harry **complained**. "Maybe there's no place like home ... unless maybe the best part of this year was traveling so much?" Harry wondered. And so it was that this **traveler** decided to explore all of Europe, make new friends, and learn many languages until he found his true home.

Questions:

1. ¿A qué continente se mudó Harry? _____

   Which continent did Harry move to?

2. ¿Qué clase de personas encontró Harry en España? _____

   What kind of people did Harry find in Spain?

3. ¿Qué ropa usaba Harry en Finlandia? _____

   What clothes did Harry wear in Finland?

4. ¿Cómo eran las personas en Finlandia? _____

   How were people in Finland?

5. ¿Cuál fue el último país que Harry visitó? _____

   Which was the last country Harry visited?

6. ¿Cuál fue la mejor parte del año? _____

   Which was the best part of the year?

Answers:

1.

    a. Yo estoy caminando rápido.

    b. Tú estás estudiando francés.

    c. Él está saltando alto.

    d. Ella está tocando la guitarra.

    e. Usted está limpiando el piso.

    f. Nosotros estamos cantando juntos.

    g. Vosotros estáis viendo la película.

    h. Ellos están escuchando la radio.

    i. Ellas están nadando en la playa.

    j. Yo estoy rompiendo un papel.

2.

    a. aprendiendo

    b. conduciendo

    c. yendo

    d. pintando

    e. tomando

    f. construyendo

    g. bañando

    h. diciendo

    i. doblando

    j. hirviendo

3.

    a. caminando

    b. leyendo

    c. cortando

    d. peleando

    e. golpeando

    f. jugando

g. tocando

h. moviendo

i. rompiendo

j. viajando

4.

    a. ✕

    b. ✕

    c. ✓

    d. ✕

    e. ✓

    f. ✕

    g. ✓

    h. ✓

    i. ✕

    j. ✕

5.

    a. bebiendo

    b. escribiendo

    c. escuchando

    d. caminando

    e. volando

    f. comiendo

    g. viajando

    h. cocinando

    i. leyendo

    j. estudiando

Translations:

1. My mom is fixing the garden of the house.

2. The student is reading a new book.

3. You are dancing very well.

4. We are working together on this project.

5. You are eating a salad.

6. I am talking to a coworker.

7. He is dying of thirst.

8. You are not listening to me while I am talking.

9. The dog is running from one side to the other.

10. My brothers are drinking to celebrate.

Story:

1. Europa.

2. Personas que no lo aceptaban.

3. Grandes abrigos.

4. Muy amables.

5. Bélgica.

6. Viajar tanto.

Chapter 15
DIRECT OBJECT PRONOUNS

Direct object pronouns are also used in English. They are words used to replace the object that's directly affected by the verb of a sentence. To help find the Direct Object of a sentence, you may ask yourself, "what?" or "who?" See the examples below:

Louise watched the movie.
Louise watched what?
Louise watched **the movie**.

Thomas kissed Sophie.
Thomas kissed who?
Thomas kissed **Sophie**.

In this case, the subjects are Louise and Thomas, while the Direct Objects are the movie and Sophie. This lesson will teach you which pronouns to use in the place of the Direct Objects in Spanish.

Here is the list of Direct Object Pronouns you will use in Spanish:

Subject pronouns		Direct object pronouns	
I	Yo	Me	Me
You	Tú	You	Te
He, She	Él, Ella	Him, Her	Lo, La
We	Nosotros/as	Us	Nos
You	Vosotros/as	You	Os
They	Ellos/as	Them	Los, Las

The Direct Object Pronoun always has to match, in gender and quantity, the Direct Object, not the subject of the sentence. Regardless of a female, male, plural, or singular subject of the sentence, the Direct Object Pronoun has to match the Direct Object.

It's very important to remember that in Spanish, the Direct Object Pronoun is not placed at the end of the sentence like in English; it is placed right before the verb. Take a look at the examples below:

Louise watched the movie.
Louise vio la película.
Louise watched **it.**
*Louise **la** vio.*

Thomas kissed Sophie.
Thomas besó a Sophie.
Thomas kissed **her.**
*Thomas **la** besó.*

Now it's just a matter of studying the necessary examples:

- *Él**me** saludó esta mañana.* - He greeted *me* this morning.

- *Nosotros **te** compramos un regalo.* - We bought *you* a gift.

- *Usted **lo** vio en el parque.* - You saw *him* at the park.

- *Tú **nos** conoces desde hace diez años.* - You met *us* ten years ago.

- *Yo **las** llamé muchas veces esta tarde.* - I called *them* many times this afternoon.

In these examples, you can notice the most important things about Direct Object Pronouns. We make use of each of them (*me, te, lo/la, nos, os, los/las*), we observe the translations in English (*me, you, him/her, us, them*), and we place the pronouns in the correct order in the sentence, which is before the verb.

Examples:

1. Yo hice galletas, y me las comí todas.
   I made cookies, and ate them all.

2. Ella leyó el libro. Luego, lo devolvió.

   She read the book. Then, she gave it back.

3. Mis padres me llamaron por la mañana.

   My parents called me in the morning.

4. Yo los compré.

   I bought them.

5. Nosotros las vimos.

   We saw them.

Exercises:

1. Change the Direct Object in these sentences for a Direct Object Pronoun:

    a. Yo lavé las camisas.

    _____

    b. Tú compraste el cuaderno.

    _____

    c. Ella llamó al padre.

    _____

    d. Él rompió la promesa.

    _____

    e. Nosotros vimos los pájaros.

    _____

    f. Vosotros llamasteis a la secretaria.

    _____

    g. Yo conocí al policía.

    _____

    h. Tú escribiste la nota.

    _____

    i. Jorge jugó al juego.

    _____

    j. Laura no bebió vino.

    _____

2. Translate these short sentences from English to Spanish, placing the Direct Object Pronoun where it belongs in Spanish:

    a. I ate it. _____

    b. He painted it. _____

    c. We washed it. _____

    d. They met her. _____

    e. You ignored him. _____

    f. She called me. _____

    g. He found us. _____

h. I contacted them.　　　_____

i. He bought it.　　　_____

j. You drew it.　　　_____

3. Complete the sentences with the correct Direct Object Pronoun:

　　a. Yo vi a mi amigo y _____ saludé.

　　b. Esta es la escuela, _____ pintaron este mes.

　　c. Nosotros somos familia, _____ queremos mucho.

　　d. La más popular es Clara; _____ llaman muchas personas.

　　e. Mi tía compró esta camisa, _____ rompió y _____ arregló.

　　f. Ella adoptó dos perros y _____ llevó a su casa.

　　g. Alfred compró dos hamburguesas y _____ comió muy rápido.

　　h. Nosotros buscamos secretaria. _____ encontraremos pronto.

　　i. Yo lavé el plato y _____ guardé en la cocina.

　　j. Tú escuchaste esta canción y _____ aprendiste.

4. Write ✓ if the sentence uses the correct Direct Object Pronoun or ✗ if it doesn't:

　　a. Yo vendí mis zapatos y ahora los echo de menos.　　_____

　　b. Tú vas a escribir una carta y la vas a enviar.　　_____

　　c. Gregory visitará el museo y nos encantará.　　_____

　　d. Doris escribe un libro y lo comenta con todos.　　_____

　　e. Nosotros lavamos el coche y la dejamos como nuevo.　　_____

　　f. Vosotros conocéis a la profesora y no las quieren.　　_____

　　g. Ellos comen mariscos y los disfrutan mucho.　　_____

　　h. Yo vi un pingüino y nunca te olvidaré.　　_____

　　i. Yo amo el teatro, lo visito cada mes.　　_____

　　j. Emilia compró flores y las llevó a su casa.　　_____

5. Write the following sentences in English using the correct Direct Object Pronouns:

　　a. Yo los llamé.　　_____

　　b. Ella la escribió.　　_____

　　c. Nosotros lo rompimos.　　_____

　　d. Anderson me pegó.　　_____

e. Tú me viste. _____

f. Ellos te gritaron. _____

g. Él lo movió. _____

h. Yo la abracé. _____

i. Usted lo echó. _____

j. Antonia te ayudó. _____

Translations:

Translate the following sentences into English:

1. Yo fui a la playa en julio. La disfruté mucho.

_____

2. Mi primo escribió esta canción. Y la escribió solo.

_____

3. Jimena compró una blusa. En la cena, la manchó.

_____

4. Esta es mi casa; la pinté de blanco.

_____

5. No quiero hacer mi trabajo hoy. Lo quiero hacer mañana.

_____

6. Nosotros vamos a cocinar la comida y luego nos la vamos a comer.

_____

7. El perro jugó con el juguete y luego lo rompió.

_____

8. José compró unos zapatos, los usó, y los devolvió.

_____

9. El profesor escribió una carta. Al día siguiente, la envió.

_____

10. Mi madre se echó una siesta; la disfrutó mucho.

_____

Story:

El trabajo de un **crítico** de películas no es nada fácil. Para poder criticar películas, primero se tiene que estudiar mucho; se tienen que tener muchos **conocimientos** sobre el **tema**. Un crítico debería saber cómo hacer películas, saber hacer el trabajo de los directores, productores, **camarógrafos**, actores, y demás personas que hacen películas. Solo así, el crítico puede ver una película y decir: "La vi, y creo que es mala." Puede ver una película de terror y decir: "La vi, y creo que está mal hecha." Puede ver una película romántica y decir: "La vi, y creo que es de mala **calidad**."

Pero, a veces, no hay que ser un experto para ser el mejor crítico de películas. A veces, los mejores críticos son los niños. Al salir del cine, le puedes hacer preguntas a los niños y las respuestas serán **maravillosas**. Un niño dijo: "¡Vi un **fantasma**, yo le dije que se fuera de la casa, y él me escuchó!". Una niña dijo: "El **príncipe** le dio un beso a la princesa, y la llevó al castillo, ¡fue perfecto!". Otro niño dijo: "El héroe entró al **edificio**, saltó, corrió, disparó y ¡les ganó a todos! ¡Así seré yo algún día!". Al final del día, lo más importante es **disfrutar** las películas como cuando éramos niños.

Vocabulary List:

1. crítico – critic
2. conocimientos - knowledge
3. tema - subject
4. camarógrafos - cameramen
5. calidad - quality
6. maravillosas - wonderful
7. fantasma - ghost
8. príncipe - prince
9. edificio - building
10. disfrutar - enjoy

Translated Story:

The job of a movie **critic** is not an easy one. To be able to criticize movies, you first have to study a lot; you have to have a lot of **knowledge** about the **subject**. A critic should know how to make movies and know how to do the work of directors, producers, **cameramen**, actors, and other people who make movies. Only then can the critic see a movie and say, "I saw it, and I think it's bad"." He can watch a horror movie and say, "I saw it, and I think it was poorly done"." He can watch a romance movie and say, "I saw it, and I think it's of bad **quality**."

But sometimes, you don't have to be an expert to be the best movie critic. Sometimes the best critics are children. When leaving the cinema, you can ask the children questions and the answers will be **wonderful**. One child said, "I saw a **ghost**; I told him to get out of the house, and he listened to me!" One girl said, "The **prince** kissed the princess, and took her to the **castle**; it was perfect!" Another child said, "The hero entered the **building**, jumped, ran, shot, and beat everyone! This is how I will be one day!" At the end of the day, the most important thing is to **enjoy** movies like when we were children.

Questions:

1. ¿Cómo es el trabajo de un crítico? _____

   What is a critic's job like?

2. ¿Qué tiene que tener un crítico? _____

   What does a critic need to have?

3. ¿Quiénes hacen las películas? _____

   Who makes the movies?

4. ¿Quiénes son los mejores críticos? _____

   Who are the best critics?

5. ¿Cómo son las respuestas de los niños? _____

   How are the children's answers?

6. ¿Qué es lo más importante? _____

   What is the most important thing?

Answers:

1.

    a. Yo las lavé.

    b. Tú lo compraste.

    c. Ello lo llamó.

    d. Él la rompió.

    e. Nosotros los vimos.

    f. Vosotros la llamasteis.

    g. Yo lo conocí.

    h. Tú la escribiste.

    i. Jorge lo jugó.

    j. Laura no lo bebió.

2.

    a. Yo lo comí.

    b. Él lo pintó.

    c. Nosotros lo lavamos.

    d. Ellos la conocieron.

    e. Tú lo ignoraste.

    f. Ella me llamó.

    g. Él nos encontró.

    h. Yo los contacté.

    i. Él lo compró.

    j. Tú lo dibujaste.

3.

    a. lo

    b. la

    c. nos

    d. La

    e. la, la

    f. los

g. las

h. La

i. lo

j. la

4.

a. ✗

b. ✓

c. ✗

d. ✓

e. ✗

f. ✗

g. ✓

h. ✗

i. ✓

j. ✓

5.

a. I called them.

b. She wrote it.

c. We broke it.

d. Anderson hit me.

e. You saw me.

f. They yelled at you.

g. He moved it.

h. I hugged her.

i. You flew it.

j. Antonia helped you.

Translations:

1. I went to the beach in July. I enjoyed it a lot.

2. My cousin wrote this song. And he wrote it alone.

3. Jimena bought a blouse. At dinner, she stained it.

4. This is my house; I painted it white.

5. I don't want to do my job today. I want to do it tomorrow.

6. We are going to cook the food and then we are going to eat it.

7. The dog played with the toy and then broke it.

8. José bought some shoes, used them, and returned them.

9. The teacher wrote a letter. The next day, he sent it.

10. My mom took a nap; she enjoyed it a lot.

Story:

1. Nada fácil.

2. Muchos conocimientos sobre el tema.

3. Directores, productores, camarógrafos y actores.

4. Los niños.

5. Maravillosas.

6. Disfrutar las películas como cuando éramos niños.

Chapter 16
INDIRECT OBJECT PRONOUNS

After learning about Direct Object Pronouns, the rational next step is to learn about Indirect Object Pronouns. Considering they are similar, it's not a very difficult subject, but it does involve an added level of complexity. It's very important that you first make sure you understand Direct Object Pronouns.

Firstly, we have to learn to identify the Indirect Object in a sentence. We know that the Direct Object is directly affected by the verb of the sentence. Now, the Indirect Object gives us important information about what will happen next to the Direct Object and where it goes. To help you locate the Indirect Object, you may ask yourself, "To whom?" or "For whom?" about the Direct Object. Let's observe this in an example.

Henry makes cookies for Nelly.

Henry makes cookies **for whom?**

For Nelly - Indirect Object

Henry hace galletas para Nelly.

Henry hace galletas **¿para quién?**

Para Nelly - Indirect Object

Very often, when the Indirect Object is obvious or has been mentioned before in the conversation, it is exchanged for a pronoun.

Here is the list of Indirect Object Pronouns used in Spanish:

Subject pronouns		Indirect object pronouns	
I	Yo	Me	Me
You	Tú	You	Te
He, She	Él, Ella	Him, Her	Le
We	Nosotros/as	Us	Nos
You	Vosotros/as	You	Os
They	Ellos/as	Them	Les

Let's see how to apply these Indirect Object Pronouns to a sentence:

- Yo **les** compré regalos de Navidad. - I bought **them** Christmas gifts.

- Tú **me** sorprendiste con esta visita. - You surprised **me** with this visit.

- Ella **nos** va a cantar una canción. - She is going to sing **us** a song.

- Nosotros **te** invitamos a ir a la fiesta. - We invite **you** to go to the party.

- Ellos **le** ayudaron a estudiar para el examen. - They helped **him/her** study for the test.

- Ella **os** castigó sin salir. – She punished **you** without going out.

Here are a few things to consider on the subject of Indirect Object Pronouns:

- The Indirect Object Pronoun always goes before the verb of the sentence, unlike in English, where it goes right after.

- "Le" and "Les" can be a little confusing, as they can refer to masculine, feminine, or you-formal objects. It has to be guessed or interpreted according to the context of the sentence.

- Sometimes, the Direct Object will not appear in a sentence as it has been previously understood.

<u>Examples:</u>

1. Yo te doy un abrazo.

    I give you a hug.

2. Él le compró un ramo de rosas.

    He bought her a bouquet of roses.

3. Tulio nos regaló una pizza.

    Tulio gifted us a pizza.

4. La cantante le dedicó una canción.

    The singer dedicated a song to him.

5. Vosotras me llamasteis por la mañana.

    You called me in the morning.

<u>Exercises:</u>

1. Change the Indirect Object of each sentence for the appropriate pronoun:

    a. Yo escribí una carta para ti.

    _____

    b. Él cantó una canción para su novia.

    _____

    c. Mi abuela hizo un jersey para mí.

    _____

    d. El chef cocinó un plato para nosotros.

    _____

    e. Ellos lavaron el coche para mi padre.

    _____

    f. Tú hiciste un pastel para ellos.

    _____

    g. Pablo plantó un árbol para el abuelo.

    _____

    h. Ella compró un vestido para mí.

    _____

    i. Usted hizo una foto para ellas.

    _____

    j. Yo pinté un cuadro para ella.

    _____

2. Translate these sentences to Spanish using the correct Indirect Object Pronouns:

    a. She played her a song.

    b. I made them a promise.

    c. You found them a friend.

    d. She told him a lie.

    e. Mathias drew her portrait.

    f. We read him poetry.

    g. They taught you Italian.

    h. He wrote me a note.

i. You showed her a movie.

j. I baked them a cake.

3. Underline the Indirect Object in these sentences:

   a. Tú das un abrazo a tu madre.

   b. Nelson abre la puerta para mí.

   c. Ellos hacen un baile para nosotras.

   d. Yo busco un novio para Andrea.

   e. Karina calienta la sopa para él.

   f. Nosotros cerramos la ventana para la abuela.

   g. Usted dice la verdad por sus hijos.

   h. Ellas enseñan inglés a los niños.

   i. Julio fabrica un juguete para mí.

   j. Tú ganas un premio para tu esposa.

4. Write the correct Indirect Object Pronoun according to the word in parenthesis:

   a. Ella (él) _____ manda saludos.

   b. Yo (nosotros) _____ compré un coche.

   c. Tú (yo) _____ presentaste la profesora.

   d. Ramón (usted) _____ entregará un mensaje.

   e. Nosotros (tú) _____ haremos una llamada.

   f. Él (Juana) _____ dará un beso.

   g. Vosotras (los perros) _____ llevareis juguetes.

   h. Isabel (yo) _____ horneo un pastel.

   i. Yo (usted) _____ hice una pregunta.

   j. Ellos (el abuelo) _____ contaron un cuento.

5. Connect the sentences in the first column with the correct translation on the right:

a. Yo les compré regalos.   1. I bought you gifts.

b. Ella les escribió cartas.   2. She wrote them letters.

c. Él les cantó canciones.   3. You sang him songs.

d. Ella me escribió cartas.   4. I bought them gifts.

e. Tú le hiciste un pastel.   5. We made ourselves a cake.

f. Yo te compré regalos.   6. I made you a cake.

g. Nosotros nos hicimos un pastel. 7. He sang them songs.

h. Usted le cantó canciones.   8. She wrote me letters.

i. Ellos me hicieron un pastel.   9. They made me a cake.

j. Yo te hice un pastel.   10. You made him a cake.

Translations:

Translate the following sentences into English:

1. Mi padre me dio un consejo muy bueno.

_____

2. La lluvia nos arruinó los planes del día.

_____

3. Tu jefe te pidió que trabajaras mañana.

_____

4. Celeste le dará un gran regalo de cumpleaños.

_____

5. Yo les dije que no podía ir a la fiesta del viernes.

_____

6. Ellos nos van a llevar al parque esta tarde.

_____

7. El gato no te escucha cuando hablas.

_____

8. Nosotros le pediremos ayuda porque es un experto.

_____

9. Benito me construyó una casa en el árbol.

_____

10. Ellas te escribieron una canción especial.

_____

Story:

Hace muchos años atrás, en un pequeño **reino** de Europa, vivía una princesa **triste**. La princesa llevaba ya diez años muy triste, porque sus padres, el rey y la reina, habían **desaparecido**. Los padres de la princesa dejaron el reino un día, y nunca volvieron. Se suponía que sería un **viaje** corto, una pequeña visita a un reino vecino, pero pasaron días, semanas, meses, y años, y los reyes no volvieron. Todas las personas del reino estaban muy **preocupadas**. Todos echaban de menos a los reyes, pero la mayor preocupación era la tristeza de la princesa.

Poco después de que se cumplieran diez años desde la desaparición de los reyes, fue el cumpleaños de la princesa. Todo el reino trabajó muy **duro** por sorprenderla con todo tipo de regalos para hacerla feliz. Los **granjeros** le regalaron las más dulces frutas y las más hermosas flores. Los caballeros le regalaron muchas **joyas**, pinturas y esculturas de la mejor calidad. Nada funcionaba. No hasta que llegó la mejor amiga de la princesa, acompañada de los más **leales** caballeros, quienes la acompañaron en una **búsqueda** secreta … ¡Habían encontrado a los reyes desaparecidos! Era un milagro. La princesa nunca más volvería a estar tan triste, y nunca olvidaría la generosidad de todos en su reino.

Vocabulary List:

1. reino – kingdom
2. triste - sad
3. desaparecido - disappeared
4. viaje - trip
5. preocupadas - worried
6. duro - hard
7. granjeros - farmers
8. joyas - jewels
9. leales - loyal
10. búsqueda - search

Translated Story:

Many years ago, in a small **kingdom** in Europe, there lived a **sad** princess. The princess had been very sad for ten years because her parents, the King and Queen, had **disappeared**. The princess's parents left the kingdom one day and never came back. It was supposed to be a short **trip**, a little visit to a neighboring kingdom, but days, weeks, months, and years passed, and the monarchs did not return. All the people in the kingdom were very **worried**. Everyone missed the monarchs, but the biggest concern was the sadness of the princess.

Shortly after ten years had passed since the disappearance of the kings, the princess had her birthday. The whole kingdom worked very **hard** to surprise her with all kinds of gifts to make her happy. The **farmers** gave her the sweetest fruits and the most beautiful flowers from her. Her knights gave her many **jewels**, paintings, and sculptures of the best quality. Nothing worked. Not until the princess's best friend arrived, accompanied by the most **loyal** knights, who accompanied her on a secret **search** ... had they found the missing monarchs! It was a miracle. The princess would never be so sad again, and she would never forget the generosity of everyone in her kingdom.

Questions:

1. ¿Quién estaba muy triste? _____

   Who was very sad?

2. ¿Quién desapareció? _____

   Who disappeared?

3. ¿Cómo estaban las personas del reino? _____

   How were the people in the kingdom?

4. ¿Qué regalos trajeron los granjeros? _____

   Which gifts did the farmers bring?

5. ¿Qué regalos trajeron los caballeros? _____

   Which gifts did the knights bring?

6. ¿Quién encontró al rey y la reina? _____

   Who found the king and the queen?

Answers:

1.

    a. Yo **te** escribí una carta.

    b. Él **le** cantó una canción.

    c. Mi abuela **me** hizo un jersey.

    d. El chef **nos** cocinó un plato.

    e. Ellos **le** lavaron el coche.

    f. Tú **les** hiciste un pastel.

    g. Pablo **le** plantó un árbol.

    h. Ella **me** compró un vestido.

    i. Usted **les** hizo una foto.

    j. Yo **le** pinté un cuadro.

2.

    a. Ella le tocó una canción.

    b. Yo te hice una promesa.

    c. Tú les encontraste un amigo.

    d. Ella le dijo una mentira.

    e. Mathias le dibujó su retrato.

    f. Nosotros le leímos poesía.

    g. Ellos te enseñaron italiano.

    h. Él me escribió una nota.

    i. Tú le enseñaste una película.

    j. Yo les horneé un pastel.

3.

    a. tu madre

    b. mí

    c. nosotras

    d. Andrea

    e. él

    f. la abuela

g. sus hijos

h. los niños

i. mí

j. tu esposa

4.

a. le

b. nos

c. me

d. le

e. te

f. le

g. les

h. me

i. le

j. le

5.

a. a-4

b. b-2

c. c-7

d. d-8

e. e-10

f. f-1

g. g-5

h. h-3

i. i-9

j. j-6

Translations:

1. My dad gave me really good advice.

2. The rain ruined our plans for the day.

3. Your boss asked you to work tomorrow.

4. Celeste will give him a great birthday gift.

5. I told them I couldn't go to the party on Friday.

6. They will take us to the park this afternoon.

7. The cat doesn't listen to you when you talk.

8. We will ask him for help because he's an expert.

9. Benito constructed me a treehouse.

10. They wrote you a special song.

Story:

1. La princesa.

2. El rey y la reina.

3. Muy preocupados.

4. Las más dulces frutas y las más hermosas flores.

5. Muchas joyas, pinturas y esculturas de la mejor calidad.

6. La mejor amiga de la princesa.

Chapter 17
PAST IMPERFECT

It's time to learn about the **Past Imperfect** tense in Spanish. This one is a little different from the preterit tense, which is a little more common, and which you probably know by now. However, the imperfect tense is not overly complicated, and the key is to understand when to use it.

Firstly, let's quickly learn how to differentiate between the preterit and the imperfect. Let's remember what the preterit looks like:

I walked to my office.
Yo **caminé** a mi oficina.

Meanwhile, the imperfect tense looks like this:

I used to walk to my office.
Yo **caminaba** a mi oficina.

It's a different conjugation that, fortunately, is quite simple. Let's take a look:

- Verbs that end in **-ar** change the ending to:

Person	Ending	Estudiar	Caminar	Hablar
Yo	-aba	estudiaba	caminaba	hablaba
Tú	-abas	estudiabas	caminabas	hablabas
Él, Ella, Usted	-aba	estudiaba	caminaba	hablaba
Nosotros/as	-ábamos	estudiábamos	caminábamos	hablábamos
Vosotros/as	-abais	estudiabais	caminabais	hablabais
Ellos/as	-aban	estudiaban	caminaban	hablaban

Examples:

1. Tú estudiabas francés por la mañana.

   You used to study French in the morning.

2. Ellos hablaban de fútbol durante el almuerzo.

   They used to talk about soccer during lunch.

3. Nosotros nos peleábamos por cualquier cosa.

   We used to fight for any reason.

- Verbs that end in **-er** or **-ir** change the ending to:

Person	Ending	Comer	Dormir	Mover
Yo	-ía	comía	dormía	movía
Tú	-ías	comías	dormías	movías
Él, Ella, Usted	-ía	comía	dormía	movía
Nosotros/as	-íamos	comíamos	dormíamos	movíamos
Vosotros/as	-íais	comíais	dormíais	movíais
Ellos/as	-ían	comían	dormían	movían

Examples:

1. Él comía pasta todos los viernes.

   He used to eat pasta every Friday.

2. Yo dormía ocho horas cada noche.

   I used to sleep eight hours every night.

3. Vosotros movíais las cosas de su lugar.

You used to move things from their place.

- Lastly, there are three irregular verbs, ser (to be), ver (to see), ir (to go):

Person	Ser	Ver	Ir
Yo	era	veía	iba
Tú	eras	veías	ibas
Él, Ella, Usted	era	veía	iban
Nosotros/as	éramos	veíamos	íbamos
Vosotros/as	erais	veníais	ibais
Ellos/as	eran	veían	iban

Examples:

1. Tú eras mi mejor amiga en el colegio.

    You used to be my best friend in school.

2. Ellos veían esta película todos los meses.

    They used to watch this movie every month.

3. Yo iba al parque todos los días con mi perro.

    I used to go to the park every day with my dog.

Note: The verb *Ser* (to be) when referring to a state of being, is irregular (They were friends – Ellos eran amigos), but when you refer to ser as a temporary condition or location, you use the verb *Estar* (to be) and it is conjugated as any other regular verb ending in **-ar** (I was sick – Yo estaba enfermo).

Now, here are a few cases to indicate when you must use the imperfect tense:

- Actions from the past that are incomplete or that don't have a precise ending.

    Yo cocinaba la cena. – I was cooking dinner.

- Actions that happened repeatedly or regularly in the past

    Tú visitabas el museo todas las semanas. – You visited the museum every week.

- Actions that precede another that took place in the past.

    Él trabajaba aquí cuando conoció a María. – He worked here when he met María.

- Describing something or someone from the past.

    La playa era hermosa. – The beach was beautiful.

- Talking about a person's age, or the time of the day.

    Ellas tenían treinta años. – They were thirty years old.

Lastly, there are a series of common sentences that usually are a sign one is talking in imperfect tense. You will learn all of them with time and practice. Here are the most commonly used ones:

- a menudo – often
- a veces – sometimes
- cada día/semana/mes/año – every day/week/month/year
- con frecuencia/frecuentemente – frequently
- muchas veces – many times
- mucho – a lot
- nunca – never
- siempre – always

Note: There is the verb "*Soler*," which means "to be used to" (in the habit of). It is conjugated like verbs that end in **-er** and placed before the verb of a sentence (I used to play guitar. – Yo solía tocar guitarra.)

Examples:

1. Vosotros siempre ibais a la playa en verano.

You always went to the beach in summer.

2. Camila nadaba en la piscina cuando empezó a llover.

    Camila was swimming in the pool when it started raining.

3. Mi abuela pintaba hermosos cuadros.

218

My grandmother painted beautiful pictures.

4. El profesor estaba enfermo la semana pasada.

   The teacher was sick last week.

5. Yo solía dormir toda la noche.

   I used to sleep all night.

Exercises:

1. Change these sentences from the past preterit to the past imperfect:

   a. Vosotros hicisteis ejercicio juntos.

   _____

   b. Él cantó canciones nuevas.

   _____

   c. Yo compré ropa europea.

   _____

   d. Nosotros pintamos toda la casa.

   _____

   e. Mi madre llamó a mi tía todo el tiempo.

   _____

   f. La doctora trabajó toda la noche.

   _____

   g. Tú bebiste zumo de naranja constantemente.

   _____

   h. El libro terminó muy bien.

   _____

   i. Usted limpió la mesa.

   _____

   j. Ellos vieron la película a menudo.

   _____

2. Write the following verbs in the past imperfect tense, according to the word in parenthesis:

   a. (Yo) Bailar   _____

   b. (Vosotras) Morir   _____

   c. (Tú) Mirar   _____

   d. (Ella) Volar   _____

   e. (Nosotros) Beber   _____

   f. (Yo) Bañar   _____

   g. (El) Decir   _____

   h. (Tú) Tener   _____

i. (Usted) Vender   _____

j. (Nosotros) Tocar   _____

3. Choose the correct conjugation to write these sentences in past imperfect tense:

   a. Ella caminaba/caminar una hora todos los días.

   b. Yo cociné/cocinaba pasta los viernes.

   c. Tú escribirás/escribías cartas para mí.

   d. Él limpiaba/limpió el baño de la casa.

   e. Yo canté/cantaba aquí muchas veces.

   f. Vosotros abríais/abriréis la tienda cada semana.

   g. Nosotros viajábamos/viajar frecuentemente.

   h. Tú correr/corrías muy rápido.

   i. El policía despertarse/despertaba temprano diariamente.

   j. Usted enseñó/enseñaba a los niños a escribir.

4. Translate these sentences to past imperfect in Spanish:

   a. We gave Spanish classes.

   _____

   b. You drew daily.

   _____

   c. I listened to music all the time.

   _____

   d. He sent messages sometimes.

   _____

   e. The dogs ran in the park.

   _____

   f. She laughed a lot.

   _____

   g. I frequently talked with Fabian.

   _____

   h. We made cookies regularly.

   _____

   i. The musician went there often.

j. He never used to invite me.

5. Write the infinitive form in Spanish of all these verbs in past imperfect form:

    a. Cerraba   _____

    b. Vendías   _____

    c. Eliminaban   _____

    d. Ibas   _____

    e. Medían   _____

    f. Lloraba   _____

    g. Reías   _____

    h. Nacían   _____

    i. Oías   _____

    j. Prometía   _____

Translations:

Translate the following sentences into English:

1. Sebastián estudiaba francés todos los viernes.

_____

2. Mi abuelo solía ir a la iglesia todos los domingos.

_____

3. Tú escribías un libro sobre la historia de tu familia.

_____

4. Yo trabajaba toda la mañana y hacía ejercicio por la tarde.

_____

5. Nosotros pedíamos dinero para pintar la escuela.

_____

6. Usted caminaba por el parque frecuentemente.

_____

7. Julia viajaba a España cada año.

_____

8. Ella hacía los deberes cuando su mejor amiga la llamó.

_____

9. El actor iba a una fiesta diferente cada fin de semana.

_____

10. Yo leía mi libro favorito sentada en esta silla.

_____

Story:

Todos hemos visto alguna vez una película de **espías**. Estas películas son muy emocionantes y están llenas de acción. Sin embargo, estas películas pueden ser muy **engañosas**. Por un lado, nos hacen **creer** cosas sobre los espías que simplemente no son ciertas. Pero, por otro lado, pueden hacernos dudar que los espías existan. ¡Oh, pero claro que existen! Hay espías en todo el mundo. Los espías son parte de la historia de la humanidad. Y es **suficiente** con interrogar a un espía para descubrir que sus vidas no son como una película, pero sí son muy interesantes e **inusuales**.

En una **entrevista** con un espía, cuyo nombre no podemos **mencionar**, el espía dio las siguientes respuestas.

"¿Cuál es la parte más emocionante de tu trabajo?" preguntamos.

"La **salida**. Cuando termino un trabajo y tengo que escapar antes de que alguien me pueda **atrapar**," respondió el espía.

La siguiente pregunta fue: "¿Cuál es la parte más aburrida de tu trabajo?"

Y el espía respondió: "**Esperar**. A veces lo único que tengo que hacer es estar en un lugar, en silencio y sin moverme por mucho tiempo."

Finalmente, al preguntar sobre su parte favorita del trabajo, el espía dijo, "¡Todas las cosas que aprendo y los lugares que visito! En cada país que visitaba, yo aprendía el idioma, era fascinante."

Vocabulary List:

1. espías – spies
2. engañosas - misleading
3. creer - to believe
4. suficiente - enough
5. inusuales - unusual
6. entrevista - interview
7. mencionar - to mention
8. salida - exit
9. atrapar - to catch
10. esperar - to wait

Translated Story:

We all have seen at some time a movie about **spies**. These movies are very exciting and are filled with action. However, these movies can be very **misleading**. On the one hand, they make us **believe** things about spies that are simply not true. But, on the other hand, they can make us doubt that spies exist. Oh, but of course they exist! There are spies all over the world. Spies are part of humanity's history. And it is **enough** to interrogate a spy to discover that their lives are not like a movie, but they are very interesting and **unusual**.

In an **interview** with a spy whose name we can't **mention**, the spy gave the following answers.

"What is the most exciting part of your job?" we asked.

"The **exit**. When I finish a job and I have to escape before someone can **catch** me," the spy answered.

The next question was: "What is the most boring part of your job?"

And the spy answered: **"Waiting**. Sometimes the only thing I have to do is be in a place, in silence and without moving for a long time."

Finally, when asked about his favorite part of the job, the spy said, "All the things I learn and the places I visit! In every country I visited, I learned the language; it was fascinating."

Questions:

1. ¿Cómo son las películas de espías? _____

   What are spy movies like?

2. ¿Qué cosas pueden ser engañosas? _____

   What things can be misleading?

3. ¿Dónde hay espías? _____

   Where are there spies?

4. ¿El nombre de quién no se puede mencionar? _____

   Whose name can't be mentioned?

5. ¿Cuándo es la salida de un espía? _____

   When is the exit of a spy?

6. ¿Por qué es aburrido esperar para un espía? _____

   Why is waiting boring for a spy?

Answers:

1.

     a. Vosotros hacíais ejercicio juntos.

     b. Él cantaba canciones nuevas.

     c. Yo compraba ropa europea.

     d. Nosotros pintábamos toda la casa.

     e. Mi madre llamaba a mi tía todo el tiempo.

     f. La doctora trabajaba toda la noche.

     g. Tú tomabas zumo de naranja constantemente.

     h. El libro terminaba muy bien.

     i. Usted limpiaba la mesa.

     j. Ellos veían la película a menudo.

2.

     a. Bailaba

     b. Moríais

     c. Mirabas

     d. Volaba

     e. Bebíamos

     f. Bañaba

     g. Decía

     h. Tenías

     i. Vendía

     j. Tocábamos

3.

     a. caminaba

     b. cocinaba

     c. escribías

     d. limpiaba

     e. cantaba

     f. abríais

g. viajábamos

h. corrías

i. despertaba

j. enseñaba

4.

    a. Nosotros dábamos clases de español.

    b. Tú dibujabas diariamente.

    c. Yo escuchaba música todo el tiempo.

    d. Él enviaba mensajes a veces.

    e. Los perros corrían en el parque.

    f. Ella reía mucho.

    g. Yo hablaba frecuentemente con Fabian.

    h. Nosotros hacíamos galletas regularmente.

    i. El músico iba ahí a menudo.

    j. Él nunca me invitaba.

5.

    a. Cerrar

    b. Vender

    c. Eliminar

    d. Ir

    e. Medir

    f. Llorar

    g. Reír

    h. Oír

    i. Prometer

Translations:

1. Sebastián used to study French every Friday.

2. Mi grandfather used to go to church every Sunday.

3. You were writing a book about your family's history.

4. I worked (used to work) all morning and exercised in the afternoon.

5. We asked (used to ask) for money to paint the school.

6. You walked (used to walk) through the park frequently.

7. Julia traveled (used to travel) to Spain every year.

8. She was doing the homework when her best friend called her.

9. The actor went (used to go) to a different party every weekend.

10. I used to read my favorite book sitting in this chair.

Story:

1. Emocionantes y están llenas de acción.

2. Las películas de acción.

3. En todo el mundo.

4. El nombre del espía.

5. Cuando termina el trabajo.

6. Porque tiene que estar en silencio y sin moverse por mucho tiempo.

Chapter 18

POR AND PARA

¿Por qué estudiar español? or *¿Para qué estudiar español?* Maybe what you're actually wondering, in this case, is, "What's the difference between *por* and *para*?" We don't blame you! It's well known that *por* and *para* are a very tricky part of learning Spanish. Basically, the confusion arises from the fact that both *por* and *para* can mean "for"; however, they also have many other meanings. Other than constant practice, the trick is to learn some of the cases when each of these is commonly used.

Por:

This word might mean - for, through, by, instead of, because of, due to, to, per, over.

These are the most common situations when *por* is used in a sentence:

- To explain the reason for doing something:

    Yo estudio historia **por** curiosidad. - I study history **because of** curiosity.

    Él faltó a trabajar **por** estar enfermo. - He skipped work **because of** being sick.

    Roberta no vio la película **por** tener miedo. - Roberta didn't watch the movie **due to** being scared.

- When you refer to the creator of something:

    Estas galletas fueron hechas por mi madre. - These cookies were made by my mom.

    El proyecto fue hecho por todos los estudiantes. - The project was done by all the students.

    El poema fue escrito por Rodolfo. - The poem was written by Rodolfo.

- When talking about the duration of an event or action:

    Yo hice ejercicio por una hora. - I exercised for one hour.

    Mi abuelo trabajó aquí por veinte años. - My grandfather worked here for twenty years.

La fiesta de graduación se extendió por tres horas. - The graduation party lasted for three hours.

- About the process of traveling or moving through, around, or by a place:

    Yo estaba caminando por el parque. - I was walking through the park.

    Nosotros viajamos por la selva amazónica. - We traveled through the Amazon jungle.

    Usted se desplazó por la autopista. - You moved along the highway.

- In questions, *¿Por qué?* means "Why?" - asking for a reason.

    ¿Por cuánto? means "For how much?" - asking for a price or amount of something.

    ¿Por dónde? means "Through where?" - asking for directions to a location.

    ¿Por cuál? means "For which?" - asking for a person or object,

    ¿Por quién? means "By whom?" - asking about the creator of a thing.

    ¿Por qué compraste esta casa? - Why did you buy this house?

    ¿Por dónde va a pasar el bus? - Where is the bus going to pass through?

    ¿Por quién fue escrito este libro? - By whom was this book written?

- *Por* is also used in popular idioms or common expressions in Spanish like: *Por ejemplo* (For example), *Por si acaso* (Just in case), *Por ciento* (percent), *Por completo* (Completely), *Por favor* (Please), *Por fin* (Finally).

    Me gustan las películas de terror. Por ejemplo, El Conjuro. – I like horror movies. For example, The Conjuring.

    Ella llevó dos abrigos, por si acaso. - She took two coats, just in case.

    Por fin pude ir a visitar a mi tía favorita. - Finally I was able to visit my favorite aunt.

- *Porque* is one word that means "Because"

    Nosotros somos amigos porque tenemos mucho en común. - We are friends because we have a lot in common.

El restaurante cerró porque el dueño se murió. - The restaurant closed because the owner died.

Tú llegaste tarde porque estaba lloviendo. - You arrived late because it was raining.

Para:

This word can mean for, by, on, to, according to, in order to

These are the most common situations when *para* is used in a sentence:

- When mentioning the final destination of a trip, journey, or process:

    Vosotros vais para Argentina. - You go to Argentina.

    Mis hijos van para casa de la abuela. - My children are going to their grandmother's house.

    Tú vas para el último piso del edificio. - You are going to the top floor of the building.

- About the recipient of something or person that something was done for:

    Ella hizo esta fiesta para Carol. - She threw this party for Carol.

    Vosotros comprasteis un teléfono para mí. - You bought a phone for me.

    Eduardo cocinó esta comida para ti. - Eduardo cooked this food for you.

- When talking about a specific date, dateline, or event in the future:

    Yo tengo que hacer los deberes para el viernes. - I have to do the homework by Friday.

    Tú tienes que completar el trabajo para mañana. - You have to finish the job for tomorrow.

    Ellos tienen que estar listos para esta tarde. - They have to be ready for this afternoon.

- When explaining the purpose or goal of doing something:

    Él cocinó la cena para impresionarte. - He cooked dinner to impress you.

Ellas van a viajar a Francia para estudiar francés. - They are going to travel to France in order to study French.

Gina toma medicina para sentirse mejor. - Gina takes medicine to feel better.

- In questions, *¿Para qué?* means "What for?" - asking for the purpose of something.

¿Para cuántos? means "For how many?" - asking for a number or amount.

¿Para dónde? Means "Where?" - asking for a destination.

¿Para cuál? means "For which?" - asking for which person or object.

¿Para quién? means "For whom?" - asking about the recipient of something.

¿Para qué sirve esta máquina? - What does this machine work for?

¿Para cuántas personas es la cena? - How many people is the dinner for?

¿Para quién es este hermoso regalo? - For whom is this beautiful gift?

Examples:

1. Yo compré estas rosas para mi novia.
   I bought these roses for my girlfriend.

2. Nosotros vamos para la playa en verano.
   We go to the beach in the summer.

3. ¿Por qué quieres ver esa película?
   Why do you want to watch that movie?

4. Ella pasó por aquí esta tarde para ir al hospital.
   She passed through here this afternoon to go to the hospital.

5. Tú no puedes ir para ese lugar.
   You can't go to that place.

Exercises:

1. Fill in the blanks with "por" or "para" according to each case:
   a. Yo no he pasado _____ aquí.
   b. Este regalo es _____ mi papa.
   c. Javier viajó _____ ocho horas.
   d. Esto no sirve _____ nada.
   e. ¿_____ dónde van a ir?
   f. Esta casa fue hecha _____ el gobierno.
   g. La película va _____ el comienzo.
   h. El cuchillo es _____ cortar.
   i. Abre la puerta, _____ favor.
   j. Tú lees este libro _____ interés propio.

2. Translate these popular expressions or phrases that include "por" or "para":
   a. Por favor _____
   b. Por ahora _____
   c. Para mí _____
   d. Para mañana _____
   e. Por completo _____
   f. Para siempre _____
   g. Por cierto _____
   h. Para ti _____
   i. Por ciento _____
   j. Por suerte _____

3. Fill the space in the parenthesis with "por" or "para," according to which word would be used in Spanish in each case:
   a. We are going to (_____) the movie theater.
   b. I am baking a pie for (_____) my wife.
   c. You will pass by (_____) the avenue.
   d. He studied economy for (_____) two years.
   e. Marcos is not going to (_____) the party.

f. The gifts are for (_____) the children.

g. She goes to the park to (_____) walk the dog.

h. They got married for (_____) true love.

i. We met because of (_____) chance.

j. The movie was made by (_____) experts.

4. Choose the right option to complete the following sentences:

    a. Yo estoy caminando

        i. por la calle.

        ii. para mí.

    b. Las flores son

        i. para Sofia.

        ii. por ellas.

    c. Él canta

        i. por pasión a la música.

        ii. para siempre.

    d. Usted va

        i. para Chile.

        ii. por favor.

    e. El hombre va

        i. por completo.

        ii. para la oficina.

    f. Ellas estudiaron juntas

        i. para el banco.

        ii. por dos años.

    g. Yo tengo que terminar los deberes

        i. para mañana.

        ii. por aquí.

    h. Nosotros vamos

        i. por el primer nivel.

        ii. para ti.

    i. Ellos van a viajar

        i. por ciento.

ii. para Francia.

j. La canción fue escrita

i. por mí.

ii. por favor.

5. Put the words in the correct order to form Spanish sentences:

a. caminaba - por - usted - plaza – la

_____

b. piano - diez - yo - por - toqué - años

_____

c. mí - madre - galletas - mi - para - hizo

_____

d. ella - aquí - por - trabajó - años - cinco

_____

e. –a – por – fue – buscar – ella – la – amor

_____

f. deberes - para - son - lunes - el - los

_____

g. peleó - él - este - por - lugar

_____

h. la - por - bus - va - el - avenida

_____

i. minutos - la - para - faltan - cena - cinco

_____

j. para - es - jabón - lavar - el

_____

Translations:

Translate the following sentences into English:

1. Yo llevé este trabajo para hacerlo en mi casa.

_____

2. El soldado pasó por muchos años de entrenamiento.

_____

3. ¿Para dónde quieres ir a comer esta noche?

_____

4. Los seres vivos necesitan oxígeno para vivir.

_____

5. Mi hijo aprendió que dos por dos es cuatro.

_____

6. Yo tengo miedo a las alturas, no puedo pasar por el puente.

_____

7. ¿Para quién es este hermoso regalo?

_____

8. Dora no puede ir a la fiesta por motivos personales.

_____

9. Juan no sabe para dónde va a ir.

_____

10. Esta escultura fue hecha por mi artista favorito.

_____

Story:

El trabajo de un policía es muy importante. Los policías deben trabajar muy duro, **arriesgar** sus vidas, y hacer todo por **proteger** las vidas de los demás **ciudadanos**. Pero es importante recordar que todos los policías también tienen vidas **privadas** fuera de sus trabajos. Estos hombres y mujeres tienen hogares, familias, **mascotas**, y hobbies que los hacen felices cuando no están trabajando. Sin embargo, a veces el trabajo y la vida privada se pueden mezclar un poco accidentalmente.

Felipe es un detective muy profesional. En su larga carrera con la policía, Felipe resolvió muchos misterios. Pero, sus casos favoritos los resolvió con su familia. No se trata de cosas horribles: son los mejores misterios. Por ejemplo, el caso de la galleta desaparecida. Todos **sospechaban** de Matías, el niño de siete años, pero la madre resultó ser la culpable. O el caso del **zapato** perdido, el cual fue **enterrado** en el jardín por un verdadero experto: el perro. Finalmente, el caso más fascinante de todos: el pastel de limón robado de la **nevera**. ¡En este caso resultó que el mismo detective fue el culpable del crimen!

Vocabulary List:

1. arriesgar - to risk
2. proteger - to protect
3. ciudadanos - citizens
4. privadas - private
5. mascotas - pets

6. sospechaban - suspected
7. culpable - guilty
8. zapato - shoe
9. enterrado - buried
10. nevera - fridge

Translated Story:

The job of a police officer is very important. Police officers must work very hard, **risk** their lives, and do everything to **protect** the lives of other **citizens**. But it's important to remember that all police officers also have **private** lives outside of their jobs. These men and women have homes, families, **pets**, and hobbies that make them happy when they are not working. However, sometimes work and private life can accidentally get a little mixed up.

Felipe is a very professional detective. In his long career with the police, Felipe solved many mysteries. But his favorite cases he solved with his family. They are not about horrible things; they are the best mysteries. For example, the case of the missing cookie. Everyone **suspected** Matías, the seven-year-old boy, but the mother turned out to be **guilty**. Or the case of the missing **shoe**, which was **buried** in the garden by a true expert, the dog. Finally, the most fascinating case of all: the lemon pie stolen from the **fridge**. In this case, it turned out that the same detective was guilty of the crime!

Questions:

1. ¿A quiénes deben proteger los policías? _____

   Who do the police officers have to protect?

2. ¿Qué cosas hacen felices a los policías? _____

   What things make the police officers happy?

3. ¿Cómo se pueden mezclar la vida privada y el trabajo? _____

   How can private life and work get mixed?

4. ¿Cuál es la profesión de Felipe? _____

   What is Felipe's profession?

5. ¿Cuántos años tiene Matías? _____

   How old is Matías?

6. ¿Quién robó el pastel de limón? _____

   Who stole the lemon pie?

Answers:

1.

     a. por

     b. para

     c. por

     d. para

     e. para/por

     f. por

     g. por

     h. para

     i. por

     j. por

2.

     a. please

     b. for now

     c. for me

     d. for tomorrow

     e. completely

     f. forever

     g. by the way

     h. for you

     i. percent

     j. luckily

3.

     a. para

     b. para

     c. por

     d. por

     e. para

     f. para

g. para

h. por

i. por

j. por

4.

    a. por la calle.

    b. para Sofia.

    c. por pasión por la música.

    d. para Chile.

    e. para la oficina.

    f. por dos años.

    g. para mañana.

    h. por el primer nivel.

    i. para Francia.

    j. por mí.

5.

    a. Usted caminaba por la plaza.

    b. Yo toqué piano por diez años.

    c. Mi madre hizo galletas para mí.

    d. Ella trabajó aquí por cinco años.

    e. Ella la fue a buscar por amor.

    f. Los deberes son para el lunes.

    g. Él peleó por este lugar.

    h. El bus va por la avenida.

    i. Faltan cinco minutos para la cena.

    j. El jabón es para lavar.

Translations:

1. I took this work to do it in my house.

2. The soldier passed through many years of training.

3. Where do you want to go to eat tonight?

4. Living beings need oxygen to live.

5. My son learned that two times two equals four.

6. I have a fear of heights; I can't go over the bridge.

7. For whom is this beautiful gift?

8. Dora can't go to the party for personal reasons.

9. Juan doesn't know where he is going to go.

10. This sculpture was made by my favorite artist.

Story:

1. A los demás ciudadanos.

2. Hogares, familias, mascotas y hobbies.

3. Accidentalmente.

4. Detective.

5. Siete años.

6. Felipe.

Chapter 19
RELATIVE PRONOUNS (QUE, QUIEN)

In English, we are very familiar with the words *who, whom, which* and *that*. They are used in sentences such as *The flowers that you planted are red.* These little words are known as **Relative Pronouns.** It is actually quite common to skip over these words in English and say *The flowers you planted are red.* However, in Spanish, they can't be ignored; they are very important. This guide will help you understand the relative pronouns in Spanish and learn how to use them.

What exactly are relative pronouns? As pronouns, they are words that stand-in for a noun. In these cases, they are related to or refer to a noun previously addressed. They are often seen as a way to connect to statements without repeating the noun. For example:

La carta es corta. - The letter is short. + *Yo escribí la carta.* - I wrote the letter.

La carta que yo escribí es corta. - The letter that I wrote is short.

La mesa está en el cuarto. - The table is in the room. + *La mesa es azul.* - The table is blue.

La mesa que está en el cuarto es azul. - The table that is in the room is blue.

The relative pronouns we're going to use in Spanish are *que* and *quien*. They not only can't be ignored in a sentence, but they require a lot of practice and study. They are very common little words, and their placement in a sentence is quite significant.

Que is the most common one, as it can be used in reference to people, things, places, and anything in between.

La comida que hice está muy buena. - The food (that) I made is very good.

La casa que compramos es grande. - The house (that) we bought is big.

Meanwhile, *Quien* is exclusively used to talk about a person. Plus, there is a plural form for this last relative pronoun: *Quienes* is used when the noun we are replacing is plural.

Isabela es quien va a ser mi esposa. - Isabela is who's going to be my wife.

Enrique es quien va a ser el profesor. - Enrique is who's going to be the teacher.

When using relative pronouns, it is very important to pay attention to the prepositions and articles that have to go before the relative pronoun. For example:

*Yo voy **a la** fiesta.* - I am going to the party. + *La fiesta es grande.* - The party is big-

Incorrect: *La fiesta que voy es grande.*

Correct: *La fiesta **a la** que voy es grande.*

Los hombres son mis amigos. - The men are my friends + *Visitamos a los hombres.* - We visited the men.

Incorrect: *Los hombres al que visitamos son mis amigos.*

Correct: *Los hombres **a los** que visitamos son mis amigos.*

Examples:

1. La casa **que** está en la montaña es pequeña.
   The house **that** is on the mountain is small.

2. Ella es **quien** ganó el primer lugar.
   She is **who** won the first place.

3. La pintura **que** hiciste es hermosa.
   The painting **that** you did is beautiful.

4. Tú encontraste el libro **que** era mío.
   You found the book **that** was mine.

5. Este es el hombre **que** arregló mi coche.
   This is the man **that** fixed my car.

6. Héctor es **quien** envió el regalo.
   Hector is **who** sent the gift.

7. Mi hijo es **quien** se mudó a Argentina.

My son is **who** moved to Argentina.

8. El vaso **que** se rompió era de vidrio.

   The glass **that** broke was glass.

9. Mi vecina es **quien** te llamó esta mañana.

   My neighbor is **who** called you this morning.

10. Este es el video de música **que** él grabó.

    This is the music video **that** he recorded.

Exercises:

1. Form a complete sentence using a relative pronoun to combine two statements:

    a. El regalo está aquí + Tú compraste el regalo

    _____

    b. El libro es de terror + Yo estoy leyendo el libro

    _____

    c. El doctor se llama Víctor + El doctor tiene bigote

    _____

    d. Mi amiga vive en Madrid + Yo echo de menos a mi amiga

    _____

    e. El colegio es grande + Yo fui a este colegio

    _____

    f. La playa es famosa + Nosotros vamos a la playa

    _____

    g. El jefe se llama Manuel + El jefe es muy estricto

    _____

    h. El teatro está lleno + Vosotros estáis en el teatro

    _____

    i. Mi prima se va a casar + Yo amo a mi prima

    _____

    j. La película dura dos horas + Te gusta la película

    _____

2. Fill in the blanks with articles/prepositions that match the number and gender of the noun:
   (en, a, a la, a las, al, a los)

    a. La reunión _____ que voy es importante.

    b. El coche _____ que viajé era muy rápido.

    c. La mujer _____ que visité es una vieja amiga.

    d. La señora _____ quien abracé es mi abuela.

    e. Los niños _____ que llamé son mis primos.

    f. El problema _____ que estamos es complicado.

    g. El hotel _____ que llegué era de cinco estrellas.

247

h. El lugar _____ que vamos es muy famoso.

i. Las plantas _____ que regué van a crecer.

j. Los perros _____ que adopté son felices.

3. Translate these English sentence where the relative pronoun is omitted into Spanish sentences with a relative pronoun:

a. The rose you gave me died.

_____

b. The friend he remembers has changed.

_____

c. The cookies I made are sweet.

_____

d. That man you met is a liar.

_____

e. The song she sang made me cry.

_____

f. The women we met are all good friends.

_____

g. The picture you saw is really old.

_____

h. The class we're going to is at 7 am.

_____

i. The door you closed is locked now.

_____

j. The job I accepted is too difficult.

_____

4. Write two separate sentences in Spanish from the following statements, taking away the relative pronoun that links them together.

a. Las casas que ellos construyeron están listas.

_____

b. El tatuaje que me hice dolió mucho.

_____

c. La ceremonia a la que nos invitaron es hoy.

_____

d. Los anillos que ella compró son de oro.

_____

e. El estudiante que tiene el libro lo está leyendo.

_____

f. Las cartas que tú enviaste las guardé.

_____

g. Mis hermanos a los que echo de menos viven en México.

_____

h. La profesora que da esta clase es Maribel.

_____

i. El barco en que viajamos es muy lujoso.

_____

j. Las paredes que pintamos ya se secaron.

_____

5. Mark the following sentences with a ✓ if they're written correctly, and with a ✗ if they are
   wrong:
   a. Mi primo que tiene 23 años se graduó.   _____
   b. El bolso a quien compré es azul.   _____
   c. Los deberes que tienes que hacer son difíciles _____
   d. El baño a los que tomé fue relajante.   _____
   e. La llamada al que contestaste fue corta.   _____
   f. El edificio en que vivo tiene diez pisos.   _____
   g. Las manzanas que comimos eran rojas.   _____
   h. Los amigos a quienes vi son españoles.   _____
   i. La comida en que ella cocinó fue perfecta.   _____
   j. El baile al quien aprendimos es fácil.   _____

Translations:

Translate the following sentences into English:

1. La historia que escribí ganó un premio en literatura.

_____

2. Esta es mi amiga de quien te había hablado tanto.

_____

3. La oficina a la que fuiste no era la correcta.

_____

4. Este cantante no es quien escribió tu canción favorita.

_____

5. La camisa que llevas puesta es muy elegante.

_____

6. Mi primo es quien me enseñó a hablar francés.

_____

7. Estas son las cartas que mi padre le escribió a mi madre.

_____

8. Yo voy al museo en el que se encuentra esta escultura.

_____

9. Usted aún no conoce a las personas con quienes va a trabajar.

_____

10. Habrá un premio para quien llegue primero al final.

_____

Story:

Esta es la historia de una mujer llamada Victoria, quien era increíblemente **ambiciosa** y **trabajadora**. Desde que era tan solo una niña, Victoria trabajó más duro que todas las personas a su **alrededor**. Victoria finalmente se convirtió en la mejor estudiante de su clase y de todo el colegio. No fue una sorpresa para nadie que una prestigiosa universidad le ofreciera una **beca** a Victoria. Y, para ser sinceros, tampoco fue una gran sorpresa que además de continuar con sus estudios, Victoria empezó a trabajar en una gran compañía. Lo que nadie se esperaba es que poco después de que Victoria consiguiera el puesto más alto en la compañía … ella simplemente **renunció**.

Todo este tiempo, el plan de Victoria era aprender todo lo posible antes de empezar su **propia** compañía. Por eso había trabajado tan duro durante tantos años. Sin embargo, cuando llegó el momento de abrir las puertas de su nueva empresa, Victoria se **dio cuenta** de que no podía hacer todo ella sola. Victoria sabía todo lo que tenía que hacer, y cómo hacerlo bien, pero tarde o temprano tuvo que **aceptar** que necesitaba ayuda. Fue la mejor decisión que pudo tomar. A partir de ese momento, Victoria pudo **relajarse**. Ya no tenía que trabajar hasta el **cansancio**. Y ahora estaba feliz de compartir su éxito con su familia y amigos.

Vocabulary List:

1. ambiciosa – ambitious
2. trabajadora - hard-working
3. alrededor - around
4. beca - scholarship
5. renunció - quit

6. propia - own
7. dio cuenta - realized
8. aceptar - to accept
9. relajarse - to relax
10. cansancio - exhaustion

Translated Story:

This is the story of a woman named Victoria, who was incredibly **ambitious** and **hard-working**. Since she was just a child, Victoria worked harder than all the people **around** her. Victoria easily became the best student in her class and in the entire school. It was no surprise to anyone that a prestigious university offered Victoria a **scholarship**. And, to be honest, it was also not a big surprise that in addition to continuing her studies, Victoria started working in a big company. What no one expected is that shortly after Victoria got the top job in the company... she just **quit**.

All this time, Victoria's plan was to learn as much as possible before starting her **own** company. That was why she had worked so hard for so many years. However, when it was time to open the doors to her new company, Victoria **realized** that she couldn't do everything on her own. Victoria knew everything she had to do and how to do it right, but sooner or later, she had to **accept** that she needed help. It was the best decision she could make. From that moment on, Victoria was able to **relax**. She no longer had to work herself to **exhaustion**. And she was now happy to share her success with her family and friends.

Questions:

1. ¿Cómo se puede describir a Victoria? _____

    How can you describe Victoria?

2. ¿Qué le ofrecieron a Victoria después del colegio? _____

    What was Victoria offered after school?

3. ¿Qué hizo Victoria cuando consiguió el puesto más alto en la compañía? _____

    _____

    What did Victoria do when she got the top job at the company?

4. ¿De qué se dio cuenta Victoria cuando abrió su propia compañía? _____

    _____

    What did Victoria realize when she opened her own company?

5. ¿Qué tuvo que aceptar Victoria? _____

    What did Victoria have to accept?

6. ¿Con quienes compartió Victoria su éxito? _____

    With whom did Victoria share her success?

Answers:

1.

    a. El regalo que compraste está aquí.

    b. El libro que estoy leyendo es de terror.

    c. El doctor que tiene bigote se llama Victor.

    d. Mi amiga a quien extraño vive en Madrid.

    e. El colegio al que fui es grande.

    f. La playa a la que vamos es famosa.

    g. El jefe que es muy estricto se llama Manuel.

    h. El teatro en que vosotros estáis está lleno.

    i. Mi prima a quien amo se va a casar.

    j. La película que te gusta dura dos horas.

2.

    a. a la

    b. en

    c. a la

    d. a

    e. a los

    f. en

    g. al

    h. al

    i. a las

    j. a los

3.

    a. La rosa que me diste murió.

    b. El amigo que él recuerda ha cambiado.

    c. Las galletas que yo hice son dulces.

    d. El hombre que conociste es un mentiroso.

    e. La canción que ella cantó me hizo llorar.

    f. Las mujeres que conocimos son todas buenas amigas.

g. La foto que viste es muy vieja.

h. La clase a la que vamos es a las 7 am.

i. La puerta que tú cerraste está atrancada ahora.

j. El trabajo que yo acepté es muy difícil.

4.

a. Las casas están listas. + Ellos construyeron las casas.

b. El tatuaje dolió mucho. + Me hice un tatuaje.

c. La ceremonia es hoy. + Nos invitaron a la ceremonia.

d. Los anillos son de oro. + Ella compró los anillos.

e. El estudiante está leyendo el libro. + El estudiante tiene el libro.

f. Las cartas las guardé. + Tú enviaste las cartas.

g. Mis hermanos viven en México. + Extraño a mis hermanos.

h. La profesora es Maribel. + Maribel da esta clase.

i. El barco es muy lujoso. + Viajamos en este barco.

j. Las paredes se secaron. + Pintamos las paredes.

5.

a. ✓

b. ✗

c. ✓

d. ✗

e. ✗

f. ✓

g. ✓

h. ✓

i. ✗

j. ✗

Translations:

1. The story that I wrote won a prize in literature.

2. This is my friend who I've talked to you about so much.

3. The office which you went to wasn't the right one.

4. This singer is not who wrote your favorite song.

5. The shirt that you're wearing is very elegant.

6. My cousin is who taught me to speak French.

7. These are the letters that my dad wrote to my mom.

8. I am going to the museum in which this sculpture is found.

9. You still don't know the people with whom you'll be working.

10. There will be a prize for who arrives at the end first.

Story:

1. Victoria era increíblemente ambiciosa y trabajadora.

2. Una beca.

3. Ella simplemente renunció.

4. Victoria se dio cuenta de que no podía hacer todo ella sola.

5. Victoria tuvo que aceptar que necesitaba ayuda.

6. Victoria compartió su éxito con su familia y amigos.

Chapter 20
PAST CONTINUOUS

Another important lesson in the journey to mastering a conversational level in Spanish is knowing how to use the **Past Continuous** tense.

For this subject, it might be useful to review previous lessons, like **Chapter 14: Present Continuous**, to review verb gerunds in Spanish, and **Chapter 17: Past Imperfect**, as we will be using terms from both chapters.

The Past Continuous is used to talk about actions or events that took place in the past but when speaking about the moment in which they were taking place. It is helpful to observe how it compares to other past tenses.

Simple Past	Past Imperfect	Past Continuous
Yo estudié	*Yo estudiaba*	*Yo estaba estudiando*
I studied	I used to study	I was studying

The structure of a Past Continuous sentence is the following:

Subject + Verb *Estar* (To be) (Simple Past) + Verb (gerund)

Ella + estaba + cocinando. (She was cooking.)

Let's remind ourselves of some important information:

- Simple Past tense of the verb *Estar*:
    - Yo estaba
    - Tú estabas
    - Él/Ella/Usted estaba
    - Nosotros/as estábamos
    - Vosotros/as estabais
    - Ellos/Ellas estaban

- Gerunds in Spanish:
    - Verbs ending in **-ar** change to **-ando:** Caminando, Bailando, Pintando
    - Verbs ending in **-ir** or **-er** change to **-iendo:** Escribiendo, Saliendo, Moviendo
    - Irregular verbs like: Leyendo, Viendo, Durmiendo.

- To form negative sentences in the Past Continuous tense, the word "no" must be placed right after the subject and before the verb *Estar*.
    - Tú no estabas en tu casa. - You were not in your house.

- Usually, the Past Continuous tense is used to introduce another action that took place in the past. This second event is written in the Simple Past tense.
    - Él estaba cantando cuando nosotros llegamos. - He was singing when we arrived.

Examples:

1. Yo estaba viajando en avión.
   I was traveling by plane.

2. Nosotros no estábamos en la clase.
   We weren't in the class.

3. Usted estaba sentado en esa silla.
   You were sitting in that chair.

4. Tony estaba jugando a fútbol.
   Tony was playing soccer.

5. Ellas estaban aprendiendo a nadar.
   They were learning how to swim.

Exercises:

1. Transform these Simple Past sentences into Past Continuous sentences in Spanish:

    a. Tú corriste por el parque.

    _____

    b. Yo vi una película de acción.

    _____

    c. Nosotros hicimos galletas.

    _____

    d. Usted fue al baño.

    _____

    e. La profesora dio la clase.

    _____

    f. Él cambió de opinión.

    _____

    g. Tú escribiste un poema.

    _____

    h. Ellos tocaron una canción.

    _____

    i. Yo hice una foto.

    _____

    j. Vosotros limpiasteis la mesa.

    _____

2. Complete these sentences writing the gerund of the verb in the parenthesis:

    a. Yo estaba (mover) _____ la mesa.

    b. Tú estabas (cerrar) _____ la ventana.

    c. Nosotros estábamos (ver) _____ una película.

    d. Él no estaba (escuchar) _____ al profesor.

    e. Usted estaba (nadar) _____ en el río.

    f. El gato estaba (tomar) _____ leche fría.

    g. El doctor estaba (atender) _____ a un paciente.

    h. Yo no estaba (dormir) _____ en la mañana.

i. Ella estaba (ganar) _____ la competencia.

j. Tú no estabas (llamar) _____ a la policía.

3. Change these Past Continuous sentences to Past Imperfect sentences in Spanish:

    a. Usted estaba caminando por la playa.

    _____

    b. Tú estabas haciendo un dibujo.

    _____

    c. Él estaba montando bicicleta.

    _____

    d. Ella estaba ayudando a los ancianos.

    _____

    e. Nosotros estábamos aprendiendo alemán.

    _____

    f. El perro estaba saltando en el jardín.

    _____

    g. Yo estaba viajando a Canadá.

    _____

    h. Mi padre estaba trabajando por la noche.

    _____

    i. Ellos estaban visitando a un amigo.

    _____

    j. Ella estaba echando una siesta.

    _____

4. Pick the right translation for each of these Past Continuous sentences:

    a. Yo estaba contando un cuento.

        i. I told a joke.

        ii. I was telling a story.

    b. Tú estabas eligiendo un vestido.

        i. I am choosing a dress.

        ii. You were choosing a dress.

    c. Él estaba yendo al banco.

    i.   He was going to the bank.

    ii.   He was yelling at the bank.

d. Usted estaba ayudando al niño.

    i.   You were helping the kid.

    ii.   You are helping the kid.

e. Nosotros estábamos tomando vino.

    i.   We were not drinking.

    ii.   We were drinking wine.

f. Carol estaba comprando un teléfono.

    i.   Carol was buying a phone.

    ii.   Carol bought a new phone.

g. Yo estaba hablando con mi tía.

    i.   I used to talk to my aunt.

    ii.   I was talking to my aunt.

h. El héroe estaba muriendo en el libro.

    i.   The hero is dying in the book.

    ii.   The hero was dying in the book.

i. Tú no estabas llorando en el funeral.

    i.   You always cry at funerals.

    ii.   You were crying at the funeral.

j. El perro estaba mirando por la ventana.

    i.   The dog was walking by the door.

    ii.   The dog was watching through the window.

5. Fill in the blanks to complete the following sentences:

  a. Yo _____ leyendo cuando perdí el libro.

  b. _____ estábamos viajando cuando se dañó el coche.

  c. Tú estabas en tu casa _____ yo llegué.

  d. Él estaba en clase cuando _____ llamaste.

  e. Tú _____ escuchando música cuando te dormiste.

  f. Nosotros _____ jugando a tenis cuando llovió.

  g. Ella estaba trabajando _____ yo renuncié.

  h. Tú estabas bailando cuando _____ te vi.

i. El perro estaba escapando cuando _____ lo atrapamos.

j. Usted _____ saliendo cuando cerraron la puerta.

Translations:

Translate the following sentences into English:

1. Nosotros estábamos en el mejor concierto del año.

_____

2. Yo estaba tomando un baño cuando sonó el teléfono.

_____

3. Usted no estaba trabajando el lunes por la mañana.

_____

4. El abogado no estaba recibiendo nuevos clientes.

_____

5. Tú estabas esperando el bus cuando empezó a llover.

_____

6. Jorge estaba conduciendo el coche cuando sonó su teléfono móvil.

_____

7. Ellos estaban hablando de ti cuando yo entré al cuarto.

_____

8. Ella estaba escribiendo un libro sobre sus viajes.

_____

9. Yo estaba haciendo ejercicio por motivos de salud.

_____

10. Mi madre estaba cocinando mi comida favorita.

_____

Story:

Laura Moreno es una reportera famosa. Ella ha trabajado para todas las **revistas** más populares y también las más prestigiosas del mundo. Laura se hizo famosa por sus preguntas originales y creativas. Además, ella siempre entrevista a las personas más interesantes, y logra hacerles **revelar** grandes secretos. Por ejemplo, cuando un reconocido aventurero admitió "Yo estaba llegando a la **cima** de montaña cuando **falló** la cámara, y decidí que no valía la pena **llegar** a la cima sin poder **grabar** mi gran momento."

En otra ocasión, Laura entrevistó a una famosa actriz que dijo: "Nosotros estábamos grabando la última escena de la película cuando se me ocurrió que mi personaje no **merecía** morir. Así que en el último momento abrí los ojos, y así termina la película: en suspense." Después de tantas reveladoras entrevistas, por fin alguien **decidió** entrevistar a Laura Moreno. Todos están de acuerdo en que la mejor parte de la entrevista fue cuando le preguntaron a la famosa reportera cuál era su **truco** para **conseguir** las mejores respuestas. Laura dijo: "Mi truco es que mantengo mi curiosidad de la infancia. Nunca me canso de preguntar, y nunca me rindo. Los niños son los mejores reporteros."

Vocabulary List:

1. revistas – magazines
2. revelar - to reveal
3. cima - top
4. falló - failed
5. llegar - to arrive

6. grabar - to record
7. merece - deserve
8. decidió - decided
9. truco - trick
10. conseguir - to get

Translated Story:

Laura Moreno is a famous reporter. She has worked for all the most popular **magazines** and for the most prestigious ones too. Laura became famous for her original and creative questions. Additionally, she always interviews the most interesting people and manages to make them **reveal** great secrets. For example, when a great adventurer admitted, "I was arriving at the **top** of the mountain when the camera **failed**, and I decided it wasn't worth it to **arrive** at the top without being able to **record** my big moment."

On another occasion, Laura interviews a famous actress who said: "We were shooting the last scene of the movie when I thought that my character doesn't **deserve** to die. So at the last moment, it was my idea to open my eyes, and that way, the movie ends in suspense." After so many revealing interviews, finally, someone decided to interview Laura Moreno. Everyone agrees that the best part of the interview was when they asked the famous reporter what her **trick** was to get the best answers. Laura said: "My trick is that I keep my curiosity from childhood. I never get tired of asking, and I never give up. Children are the best reporters."

Questions:

1. ¿Cuál es la profesión de Laura? _____

   What is Laura's profession?

2. ¿Para qué revistas ha trabajado Laura? _____

   Which magazines has Laura worked for?

3. ¿A quién le falló la cámara? _____

   Whose camera failed?

4. ¿Qué hizo la actriz en la última escena? _____

   What did the actress do in the last scene?

5. ¿A quién entrevistaron al final? _____

   Who did they interview in the end?

6. ¿Quiénes son los mejores reporteros? _____

   Who are the best reporters?

<u>Answers:</u>

1.

    a. Tú estabas corriendo por el parque.

    b. Yo estaba viendo una película de acción.

    c. Nosotros estábamos haciendo galletas.

    d. Usted estaba yendo al baño.

    e. La profesora estaba dando la clase.

    f. Él estaba cambiando de opinión.

    g. Tú estabas escribiendo un poema.

    h. Ellos estaban tocando una canción.

    i. Yo estaba haciendo una foto.

    j. Vosotros estabais limpiando la mesa.

2.

    a. moviendo

    b. cerrando

    c. viendo

    d. escuchando

    e. nadando

    f. tomando

    g. atendiendo

    h. durmiendo

    i. ganando

    j. llamando

3.

    a. Usted caminaba por la playa.

    b. Tú hacías un dibujo.

    c. Él montaba en bicicleta.

    d. Ella ayudaba a los ancianos.

    e. Nosotros aprendíamos alemán.

    f. El perro saltaba en el jardín.

g. Yo viajaba a Canadá.

h. Mi padre trabajaba por la noche.

i. Ellos visitaban a un amigo.

j. Ella tomaba una siesta.

4.

a. I was telling a story.

b. You were choosing a dress.

c. He was going to the bank.

d. You were helping the kid.

e. We were drinking wine.

f. Carol was buying a phone.

g. I was talking to my aunt.

h. The hero was dying in the book.

i. You were crying at the funeral.

j. The dog was watching through the window.

5.

a. estaba

b. Nosotros

c. cuando

d. tú

e. estabas

f. estábamos

g. cuando

h. yo

i. nosotros

j. estaba

Translations:

1. We were in the best concert of the year.

2. I was taking a bath when the phone rang.

3. You were not working on Monday morning.

4. The lawyer was not accepting new clients.

5. You were waiting for the bus when it started raining.

6. Jorge was driving the car when his cellphone rang.

7. They were talking about you when I entered the room.

8. She was writing a book about her trips.

9. I was doing exercise for health reasons.

10. My mom was cooking my favorite food.

Story:

1. Laura es una reportera.

2. Laura ha trabajado para las revistas más populares y prestigiosas del mundo.

3. Al gran aventurero le falló la cámara.

4. La actriz abrió los ojos.

5. Entrevistaron a Laura Moreno.

6. Los niños son los mejores reporteros.

Chapter 21
RECIPROCAL VERBS

In this chapter, we are going to study a very interesting subject, something that might seem a little tricky, but don't make the mistake of thinking it isn't essential. We are talking about **Reciprocal Verbs.** They are something that naturally comes up very often in conversation in Spanish. So it's important that when learning this beautiful language, you take the time to master the use of Reciprocal Verbs.

A very useful step before starting this lesson is to review a similar subject, **Reflexive Verbs**, which should be familiar now; just take a look at Chapter 4 of this guide. Reciprocal Verbs indicate that the subject of the sentence is also the object. This means that a person performs an action on themselves. To achieve this, these sentences make use of reflexive pronouns (me, te, se, and nos).

Let's take a look at a few examples:

- Yo *me* baño por la mañana. – I shower in the morning.
- Tú *te* vas a casa. - You leave the house.
- Él *se* mueve rápido. - He moves quickly.
- Nosotros *nos* vestimos bien. - We dress well.
- Vosotros *os* quejáis mucho. – You complain a lot.
- Ellas *se* duermen temprano. - They sleep early.

Once you understand this subject, you can go ahead and dive deep into Reciprocal Verbs. When we say reciprocal, we are talking about reciprocity: an equal give and take. In this case, Reciprocal Verbs are a way to show that the subjects of the sentence are doing something *to each other*, not just to themselves as individuals, but there's an exchange made. For this reason, Reciprocal Verbs are only used with *plural subjects*. For example:

Nosotros nos escribimos cartas. - We write each other letters.

This means that the people involved write letters from one to the other, not that each person writes themselves a letter. To make this distinction very clear, it is common to say *unos a otros/unas a otras/el uno al otro/la una a la otra,* which translates to "to each other."

Not all verbs can be used as Reciprocal Verbs. For this reason, we have included a list of the most frequently used Reciprocal Verbs in Spanish. Take a look:

Amarse	to love each other
Llamarse	to call each other
Escribirse	to write to each other
Conocerse	to know each other
Ayudarse	to help each other
Besarse	to kiss each other
Abrazarse	to hug each other
Verse	to see each other
Hablarse	to talk to each other

You will notice that a reciprocal verb is the infinitive form of the **verb + -se**. This will help you differentiate from non-reciprocal verbs. For example:

Ellos escriben. - They write.

Ellos se escriben. - They write to each other.

It is very different to say that two people are writing (in general), than saying they are writing to each other.

As you continue to work with Reciprocal Verbs, you'll notice they can be conjugated in different tenses, just like any other verb. For example:

- Ellas se ayudaron. - They helped each other.
- Ellas se ayudaban. - They used to help each other.
- Ellas se ayudan. - They help each other.

- Ellas se están ayudando. - They are helping each other.
- Ellas se ayudarán. - They will help each other.

Lastly, when writing negative sentences, remember to place the word "no", right after the subject, and before the reflexive pronoun and reciprocal verb:

Ellos no se conocen. - They don't know each other.

Examples:

1. Ellas se ven a menudo.
   They see each other often.

2. Nosotros nos queremos mucho.
   We love each other very much.

3. Vosotros os ayudáis el uno al otro.
   You help each other.

4. Ellos se casaron el año pasado.
   They got married last year.

5. Nosotras nos parecemos la una a la otra.
   We look like each other.

Exercises:

1. Change these basic sentences into reciprocal sentences:

    a. Ellos - escribir – poemas

    _____

    b. Vosotros - cantar – canciones

    _____

    c. Nosotros - amar – apasionadamente

    _____

    d. Ellas - llamar – semanalmente

    _____

    e. Los animales – hacer daño - sin querer

    _____

    f. Los villanos - matar - en las películas

    _____

    g. Vosotros - pelear - todo el tiempo

    _____

    h. Nosotros - observar – detenidamente

    _____

    i. Ellas - sorprender - con regalos

    _____

    j. Nosotros - ayudar - con cariño

    _____

2. Fill in the blanks with the appropriate reflexive pronoun to complete these sentences:

    a. Nosotros _____ veremos mañana.

    b. Vosotros _____ hacéis daño cocinando.

    c. Las hermanas _____ pelean todos los días.

    d. Ellos _____ despiden con un abrazo.

    e. Vosotras _____ besasteis en los labios.

    f. Los estudiantes _____ copiaron las respuestas.

    g. Nosotros _____ conocimos hace un mes.

    h. Ellas _____ abrazaron muy fuerte.

i. Vosotras _____ lleváis muy bien.

j. Nosotros _____ reunimos en mi casa.

3. Write the meaning of these Reciprocal Verbs in English:

    a. Cantarse   _____

    b. Escucharse   _____

    c. Lavarse   _____

    d. Animarse   _____

    e. Casarse   _____

    f. Matarse   _____

    g. Despedirse   _____

    h. Regalarse   _____

    i. Golpearse   _____

    j. Asustarse   _____

4. Fill in the blanks in the sentences with a Reciprocal Verb:

    a. Nosotros nos (escuchar) _____ unos a otros.

    b. Las colegas se (esperar) _____ unas a otras.

    c. Vosotros os (sorprender) _____ unos a otros.

    d. Ellos se (golpear) _____ el uno al otro.

    e. Ellas se (animar) _____ la una a la otra.

    f. Nosotros nos (ver) _____ el uno al otro.

    g. Mis primos se (abrazar) _____ el uno al otro.

    h. Nosotras nos (amar) _____ la una a la otra.

    i. Vosotros os (odiar) _____ unos a otros.

    j. Ellas se (temer) _____ unas a otras.

5. Write a Reciprocal Verb in Spanish to match these descriptions in English:

    a. to put makeup on each other   _____

    b. to bite each other   _____

    c. to kick each other   _____

    d. to destroy each other   _____

    e. to chase each other   _____

f.   to record each other   _____

g.   to pass each other   _____

h.   to scream at each other   _____

i.   to say to each other   _____

j.   to forget each other   _____

Translations:

Translate the following sentences into English:

1. Vosotras os vais a ver el próximo viernes.

_____

2. Nosotros nos besamos bajo la lluvia.

_____

3. Mis amigos no se van a divorciar todavía.

_____

4. Nosotros nos estamos mirando fijamente.

_____

5. Ellos se enfadaron por algo muy serio.

_____

6. Vosotros os peleáis los unos con los otros por cualquier cosa.

_____

7. Hace un año que vosotros os conocéis el uno al otro.

_____

8. Nosotras jamás nos haremos daño la una a la otra.

_____

9. Cada vez que ellos se ven, ellos se despiden afectuosamente.

_____

10. Nosotros nos llamamos por teléfono todos los días.

_____

Story:

En la casa de la familia Álvarez hay un secreto. Todos los **miembros** de la familia saben que hay un secreto **oculto** en la casa. El problema es que nadie sabe cómo **encontrarlo**. El gran secreto de la familia Álvarez es un álbum de fotos muy viejo. Todos saben que este álbum existe porque la abuela habla mucho de él. Por ejemplo, la abuela dice: "Deberíais ver esa **foto** en la que Juanito y Miguelito se abrazan cuando todavía usaban **pañales**." Pero nadie puede encontrar la famosa foto. Juanito y Miguelito ahora son hombres serios con hijos y nietos que pagarían por ver esa divertida foto.

Un día, toda la familia Álvarez se puso de acuerdo para buscar por toda la casa hasta encontrar el famoso álbum de fotos de la familia. Los tíos, tías, y primos se ayudaron unos a otros en esta misión. Cuando por fin encontraron el álbum de fotos en el **techo** del **ático**, todos lo celebraron, y todos se abrazaron unos a otros. Por fin toda la familia pudo reunirse para ver fotos de momentos que habían olvidado, incluyendo el **nacimiento** de Luis, el **grado** de Fernanda, y una muy divertida fiesta donde la abuela **rompió** una piñata.

Vocabulary List:

1. miembros – members
2. oculto - hidden
3. encontrarlo - find
4. foto - picture
5. pañales - diapers
6. techo - ceiling
7. ático - attic
8. nacimiento - birth
9. grado - graduation
10. rompió
11. - broke

Translated Story:

In the house of the Álvarez family, there's a secret. All the **members** of the family know there is a secret **hidden** in the house. The problem is that nobody knows how to find it. The big secret of the Álvarez family is a very old photo album. Everyone knows this album exists because the grandmother talks a lot about it. For example, the grandmother says: "You should see that **picture** where Juanito and Miguelito hugged each other when they were still wearing **diapers**." But nobody can find the famous picture. Juanito and Miguelito are serious men now with children and grandchildren that would pay to see that funny picture.

One day, the entire Álvarez family agreed to search through the entire house until they found the famous photo album of the family. The uncles, aunts, and cousins helped each other on this mission. When they finally found the photo album in the **ceiling** of the **attic**, everyone celebrated and everyone hugged each other. Finally, the entire family got together to see pictures of moments they had forgotten, including the **birth** of Luis, the **graduation** of Fernanda, and a very funny party where the grandmother **broke** a piñata.

Questions:

1. ¿Dónde hay un secreto oculto? _____

   Where's a hidden secret?

2. ¿Cuál es el gran secreto? _____

   What is the big secret?

3. ¿Quiénes pagarían por ver una foto? _____

   Who would pay to see a picture?

4. ¿Quiénes se ayudaron unos a otros? _____

   Who helped each other?

5. ¿Dónde estaba el álbum? _____

   Where was the album?

6. ¿Quién rompió una piñata? _____

   Who broke a piñata?

Answers:

1.

      a.   Ellos se escriben poemas.

      b.   Vosotros os cantáis canciones.

      c.   Nosotros nos amamos apasionadamente.

      d.   Ellas se llaman semanalmente.

      e.   Los animales se hacen daño sin querer.

      f.   Los villanos se matan en las películas.

      g.   Vosotros os peleáis todo el tiempo.

      h.   Nosotros nos observamos detenidamente.

      i.   Ellas se sorprenden con regalos.

      j.   Nosotros nos ayudamos con cariño.

2.

      a.   nos

      b.   os

      c.   se

      d.   se

      e.   os

      f.   se

      g.   nos

      h.   se

      i.   os

      j.   nos

3.

      a.   to sing to each other

      b.   to listen to each other

      c.   to wash each other

      d.   to cheer up each other

      e.   to marry each other

      f.   to kill each other

g. to say goodbye to each other

h. to give gifts to each other

i. to hit each other

j. to scare each other

4.

    a. escuchamos

    b. esperan

    c. sorprendéis

    d. golpean

    e. animan

    f. vemos

    g. abrazan

    h. amamos

    i. odiáis

    j. temen

5.

    a. maquillarse

    b. morderse

    c. patearse

    d. destruirse

    e. perseguirse

    f. grabarse

    g. pasarse

    h. gritarse

    i. decirse

    j. olvidarse

Translations:

1. You are going to see each other next Friday.

2. We kissed under the rain.

3. My friends are not going to divorce each other yet.

4. We are looking at each other intently.

5. They got angry at each other for something very serious.

6. You fight each other about anything.

7. It's been a year since you met each other.

8. We never will hurt each other.

9. Every time they see each other, they say goodbye affectionately.

10. We call each other on the phone every day.

Story:

1. En la casa de la familia Álvarez.

2. Es un álbum de fotos muy viejo.

3. Los hijos y nietos de Juanito y Miguelito.

4. Los tíos, tías, y primos.

5. En el techo del ático.

6. La abuela.

Chapter 22
SUBJUNCTIVE I

The **Subjunctive** is a very important part of the process of learning Spanish. More often than not, new learners will flinch away at the prospect of the Spanish Subjunctive. It has become a little bit of a mythical obstacle in the journey of mastering this language.

However, there's no reason to be scared or reluctant to learn this new subject. We will dedicate this chapter and the next one to making sure you feel comfortable and confident in the use of the Subjunctive. This helpful guide will touch on the most essential and useful steps to understanding and using *el subjuntivo* in Spanish.

First of all is the question, "What is the Subjunctive?" We are dealing with a "mood," not a "tense." This means we won't be working with matters of time but the intention of the sentence. To illustrate the point and introduce the Subjunctive mood, let's take a look at the three different moods we use in Spanish:

Indicative mood	Imperative mood	Subjunctive mood
Él camina deprisa.	*¡Camina deprisa!*	*Deseo que camines deprisa.*
He walks fast.	Walk fast!	I wish you would walk fast.

Here you can see how the indicative states a clear fact, the imperative expresses an order, and the Subjunctive is a wish.

The Subjunctive is more than wishes; it also includes doubts, hopes, emotions, and plans for the future, which we will study in this chapter.

Before identifying and forming full sentences with the Subjunctive mood, the first step is to see how to conjugate the verbs. Don't be intimidated by this step. The process is as follows:

- Take the infinitive form of a verb, for example, *hablar*
- Then, the first person singular form - *hablo*
- Take the letter "o" off the verb; you'll be left with the subjunctive stem: *habl-*

- Add the Subjunctive ending according to the noun:

-

Verbs that end in **-ar**		Verbs that end in **-er** or **-ir**	
Yo	-e	Yo	-a
Tú	-es	Tú	-as
Él/Ella/Usted	-e	Él/Ella/Usted	-a
Nosotros/as	-emos	Nosotros/as	-amos
Vosotros/as	-eis	Vosotros/as	-ais
Ellos/as	-en	Ellos/Ellas	-an

- Note: Be aware of irregular subjunctive stems such as:

  - haber: hay-,

  - ir: vay-,

  - saber: sep-,

  - dar: d-,

  - estar: est-,

  - ser: se-

Here you will see a few examples:

Person	Infinitive Verb	First person singular	Subjunctive
Yo	Estudiar	Estudio	Estudie
Tú	Leer	Leo	Leas
Él, Ella, Usted	Comer	Como	Coma
Nosotros/as	Escuchar	Escucho	Escuchemos
Vosotros/as	Ir	Van	
Ellos/as	Ir	Voy	Vaya

Now you are probably wondering *when* and *how* to use the subjunctive. To explain this, let's see an example:

Espero que estudies mucho. - I hope you study a lot.

There are a few important things to notice in this sentence. First, it expresses a wish, "Espero (hope)." There are two subjects in the sentence, "(**Yo**) Espero que (**tú**) estudies mucho." And there are two verbs, "**Espero** que **estudies** mucho." Notice that after the first verb, there is a "que," which goes in all subjunctive sentences. These things will help you identify and create subjunctive sentences. When there are two verbs in a sentence, and the first one expresses a wish, doubt, hope, or emotion, the second verb will be in the subjunctive.

To help, here are a few verbs and phrases that will start a subjunctive sentence:

- **For Wishes:** Querer (want), Desear (wish), Esperar (Hope), Necesitar (Need). For example:
    - Yo quiero que escuches esta canción. - I want you to listen to this song.
    - Nosotros deseamos que pasen feliz noche. - We wish you have a good night.
    - Claudia espera que todo salga bien. - Claudia hopes everything goes well.
    - Él necesita que yo lo llame. - He needs me to call him.

- **For Doubts:** Dudar (doubt), No creer (don't believe), No estar seguro (not be sure). For example:
    - Tú dudas que el concierto sea bueno. - You doubt the concert will be good.
    - Usted no cree que ellos estén en la casa. - You don't believe they are at home.
    - Ella no está segura de que seamos pareja. - She isn't sure about us being partners.

- **For emotions:** Sentir (feel), Lamentar (be sorry), Encantar (love), Sorprender (surprise). For example:
    - Kevin siente que tú no disfrutas sus fiestas. - Kevin feels you don't enjoy his parties.
    - Nosotros lamentamos que te perdieras la fiesta. - We are sorry you missed the party.

- Me encanta que vosotros cantéis esta canción. - I love that you sing this song.
- A ella le sorprende que nosotros hablemos español. - She is surprised that we speak Spanish.

Examples:

1. Yo quiero que vayamos al zoológico.

   I want us to go to the zoo.

2. Te encanta que el profesor falte a clase.

   You love that the teacher misses class.

3. Carla duda que yo cocine la cena esta noche.

   Carla doubts I'll cook dinner tonight.

4. Nosotros esperamos que ellos conozcan la ciudad.

   We hope they know the city.

5. Él desea que pintemos la casa azul.

   He wishes we paint the house blue.

Exercises:

1. Write the subjunctive form of the following verbs:

   a. Yo + trabajar   _____

   b. Ellos + bailar   _____

   c. Nosotros + morder   _____

   d. Tú + escribir   _____

   e. Ella + limpiar   _____

   f. Yo + ver   _____

   g. Usted + dormir   _____

   h. Ellas + viajar   _____

   i. Yo + aprender   _____

   j. Él + cerrar   _____

2. Fill in the blanks with one of these subjects: yo, tú, él, nosotros, vosotros:

   a. (_____) quiero que llames a la policía.

   b. Ellas quieren que (_____) vayamos a la playa.

   c. (_____) dudas que yo terminé mi carrera.

   d. Él siente que (_____) odio esta casa.

   e. Me sorprende que (_____) bailéis salsa.

   f. (_____) lamento que tengas dolor de cabeza.

   g. (_____) necesita que vosotros cambiéis de opinión.

   h. Me molesta que (_____) olvidaras mi nombre.

   i. Nosotros no creemos que (_____) compre un coche.

   j. Te encanta que (_____) limpiemos la casa.

3. Translate the first part of these sentences that express emotions:

   a. Lamento (_____) que odies este libro.

   b. Te sorprende (_____) que él conozca la canción.

   c. Nos encanta (_____) que cocines pasta.

   d. Me da miedo (_____) que el coche choque.

   e. A ella le gusta (_____) que hablemos español.

   f. Te emociona (_____) que viajemos a España.

g. A ellos les duele (_____) que ganemos el juego.

h. Nos molesta (_____) que faltes a clase.

i. Me asusta (_____) que la electricidad falle.

j. A ellas les encanta (_____) que yo baile.

4. Complete the sentences with the subjunctive form of the verb in parenthesis

   a. Deseo que tú (tener) _____ un buen día.

   b. Esperamos que vosotros (pasar) _____ un buen rato.

   c. Él no siente que ella (estar) _____ mintiendo.

   d. Tú no crees que yo (poder) _____ nadar.

   e. Vosotros teméis que ella (perder) _____ el tiempo.

   f. Quiero que nosotros (viajar) _____ el año que viene.

   g. Ella duda que usted (ser) _____ un profesional.

   h. Enrique sospecha que tú (decir) _____ la verdad.

   i. No estamos seguros de que él (hablar) _____ español.

   j. Te encanta que ellos (entrenar) _____ juntos.

5. Mark the following sentences with a ✓ if they're written correctly and with a ✗ if they are wrong:

   a. Ella desea que yo puedo volar.   _____

   b. Nosotros queremos que nos dar un aumento.   _____

   c. Me gusta que cocines comida mexicana.   _____

   d. Les sorprende que ella llegue temprano.   _____

   e. Dudas que nosotros seamos amigos.   _____

   f. Quiero que vosotros trabajo conmigo.   _____

   g. Lamentamos que tú perdimos el dinero.   _____

   h. Necesita que hagamos un plan.   _____

   i. Vosotros teméis que él caminar solo de noche.   _____

   j. No crees que yo podemos hacer los deberes.   _____

Translations:

Translate the following sentences into English:

1. Deseo que te tomes tu tiempo con este proyecto.

_____

2. Te sorprende que yo estudie español todos los días.

_____

3. Dudamos de que ella esté capacitada para este trabajo.

_____

4. Él quiere que salgamos adelante a pesar de las dificultades.

_____

5. Rosa necesita que tú le des una lista con la información.

_____

6. Usted teme que esto sea un gran engaño.

_____

7. No estoy segura de que estemos en el lugar correcto.

_____

8. Mis nietos esperan que vosotros nos visitéis más seguido.

_____

9. Te encanta que la cafetería sirva pizza para el almuerzo.

_____

10. Lamentamos que usted no pueda encontrar un trabajo que le guste.

_____

Story:

En algún momento de la historia, los trenes fueron una gran novedad. También los coches fueron algo extraordinario. Y los primeros aviones sorprendieron a toda la humanidad. Es fácil **comprender** por qué. Imagina que toda tu vida has caminado de un lugar a otro, tal vez tienes un **caballo** que te ayuda. De repente, el mundo está lleno de grandes **máquinas** que te pueden llevar al otro lado del planeta en un abrir y cerrar de ojos. Es algo increíble. Y este no es el fin de la historia. Cada día estamos más cerca de que las naves espaciales se conviertan en parte de nuestras vidas diarias. Tan solo imagen cómo serán los primeros viajes en naves espaciales:

"Bienvenidos a la nave espacial Aurora 12. En nombre de la compañía, espero que tengáis un **agradable** viaje a la luna. En nombre del resto de la humanidad, es un honor hacer este viaje con vosotros. Para **garantizar** la **seguridad** de todos los **pasajeros** y la **tripulación** a bordo de la nave espacial, por favor, necesito que todos escuchéis estas instrucciones: Todos los pasajeros deben permanecer en sus **asientos** durante el despegue. Cuando la luz pase de rojo a verde, os podréis levantar y explorar la nave. Las siguientes luces indican que podemos quitarnos los **cascos**, que la gravedad artificial ha sido activada, y que os es posible pedir bebidas y bocadillos. Gracias por escuchar."

Vocabulary List:

1. comprender - to understand
2. caballo - horse
3. máquinas - machines
4. agradable - pleasant
5. garantizar - to guarantee
6. seguridad - safety
7. pasajeros - passengers
8. tripulación - crew
9. asientos - seats
10. cascos -
11. helmets

Translated Story:

At some moment in history, trains were a great novelty. Cars were something extraordinary too. And the first planes surprised all of humanity. It's easy **to understand** why. Imagine that all your life, you have walked from one place to another; maybe you have a horse that helps you. Suddenly, the world is full of big **machines** that can take you to the other side of the planet in the blink of an eye. It is something incredible. And this is not the end of the story. Every day we are **closer** to spaceships becoming part of our daily lives. Just imagine how the first trips in spaceships will be:

"Welcome to the space ship Aurora 12. In the name of the company, I hope you have a **pleasant** trip to the moon. In the name of the rest of humanity, it is an honor to make this trip with you. To **guarantee** the **safety** of all the **passengers** and the **crew** on board of the space ship, I please need everyone to listen to these instructions. All the passengers have to remain in their **seats** during take-off. When the light passes from red to green, you will be able to get up and explore the ship. The following lights indicate that we can take off our **helmets**, as the artificial gravity was activated, and that it is possible to ask for drinks and snacks. Thank you for listening."

Questions:

1. ¿Qué métodos de transporte se mencionan primero? _____
   Which method of transportation are mentioned first?

2. ¿Qué animal te puede ayudar? _____
   What animal might help you?

3. ¿En qué se van a convertir las naves espaciales? _____
   What are spaceships going to become?

4. ¿Cuál es el destino de la nave espacial? _____
   What is the destination of the spaceship?

5. ¿De quién se debe garantizar la seguridad? _____
   Who's safety has to be guaranteed?

6. ¿Dónde deben permanecer todos durante el despegue? _____
   Where does everyone have to remain during take-off?

<u>Answers:</u>

1.

    a. Yo trabaje

    b. Ellos bailen

    c. Nosotros mordamos

    d. Tú escribas

    e. Ella limpie

    f. Yo vea

    g. Usted duerma

    h. Ellas viajen

    i. Yo aprenda

    j. Él cierre

2.

    a. Yo

    b. nosotros

    c. Tú

    d. yo

    e. vosotros

    f. Yo

    g. Él

    h. tú

    i. él

    j. nosotros

3.

    a. I am sorry

    b. You are surprised

    c. We love

    d. It scares me

    e. She likes

    f. It excites you

g. It hurts them

h. It bothers us

i. It scares me

j. They love

4.

a. tengas

b. paséis

c. esté

d. pueda

e. pierda

f. viajemos

g. sea

h. digas

i. hable

j. entrenen

5.

a. ✗

b. ✗

c. ✓

d. ✓

e. ✓

f. ✗

g. ✗

h. ✓

i. ✗

j. ✗

Translations:

1. I wish you to take your time with this project.

2. It surprises you that I study Spanish every day.

3. We doubt she's capable of this job.

4. He wants us to go on, despite the difficulties.

5. Rosa needs you to give her a list with the information.

6. You fear this is a big scam.

7. I am not sure we are in the right place.

8. My grandchildren hope you will visit us more often.

9. You love that the cafeteria serves pizza for lunch.

10. We are sorry you can't find a job you like.

Story:

1. Los trenes, los coches, y los aviones.

2. Un caballo.

3. En parte de nuestras vidas diarias.

4. La luna.

5. De todos los pasajeros y la tripulación.

6. En sus asientos.

Chapter 23
SUBJUNCTIVE II
(Giving Suggestions and Recommendations)

As we mentioned in the previous chapter, the **Subjunctive** is a big part of learning Spanish, and sometimes it can be intimidating for new students. We are confident that you had an educational and successful time working on the previous lesson. Now it's time to go a little deeper on this subject which is very well worth the two chapters we've dedicated to it.

Now we know the Subjunctive is used to express wishes, doubts, hopes, and emotions, but that's not all. In Spanish, the Subjunctive is used very often when giving suggestions and recommendations. It's important to manage the basics of working with this Spanish mood, so if you deem it necessary, take a moment to review the previous chapter and how to conjugate verbs in the subjunctive.

When giving suggestions and recommendations with the Subjunctive, it looks like this:

Yo recomiendo que compres el vestido verde. - I recommend you buy the green dress.

Just like when expressing wishes and emotions, the sentence has a few key characteristics: It has two subjects: "**Yo** recomiendo que (**tú**) compres el vestido verde." It has two verbs: "Yo **recomiendo** que **compres** el vestido verde." It has the word "que" in between the two verbs. The second verb is subjunctive, "**compres.**"

The most important part here is identifying, learning, and using the right verbs in Spanish to give suggestions and recommendations.

Here we present you with a list of the most common ones:

- *Recomendar* (to recommend):
  - Él recomienda que compres este coche. - He recommends that you buy this car.
  - Yo recomiendo que vayas al doctor. - I recommend that you go to the doctor.
  - Ellos recomendaron que veamos esta película. - They recommended we watch this movie.

- *Sugerir* (to suggest)
    - Nosotros sugerimos que viajéis en avión. - We suggest that you travel by plane.
    - Tú sugieres que trabajemos en equipo. - You suggest that we work as a team.
    - Susana sugirió que pidamos ayuda profesional. - Susana suggested we ask for professional help.

- *Aconsejar* (to advise):
    - Ellos aconsejan que no vayamos a este restaurante. - They advise that we don't go to this restaurant.
    - Yo te aconsejo que tomes un descanso. - I suggest that you take a break.
    - Usted me aconsejó que coma comida saludable. - You suggested I eat healthy food.

- *Proponer* (to propose):
    - Yo propongo que hagamos una fiesta. - I propose we have a party.
    - Ellas propusieron que brindemos por el año nuevo. - They proposed we toasted for the new year.
    - Nosotros proponemos que salgáis a caminar. - We propose that you go out to walk.

- *Decir* (to say):
    - Ella dice que veáis la serie de televisión. - She says to watch the TV show.
    - Tú dices que digamos la verdad a la policía. - You say we tell the truth to the police.
    - Usted dice que él escuche al profesor. - You tell him to listen to the teacher.

- *Insistir* (to insist):
    - Insisto en que uses un jersey esta noche. - I insist that you use a sweater tonight.
    - Carmen insiste en que invitemos a Julián. - Carmen insists we invite Julian.
    - Tú insistes en que cambiemos de ropa. - You insist we change clothes.

- There are other verbs that can be used quite often too:
    - *Animar* (to encourage)
    - *Pedir* (to ask)
    - *Rogar* (to beg)

Examples:

1. Yo digo que caminemos por el parque.

   I say we walk thought the park.

2. Gabriel recomienda que pruebes la sopa.

   Gabriel recommends you try the soup.

3. Nosotros sugerimos que usted cambie de opinión.

   We suggest you change your mind.

4. Ella aconseja que estudien español pronto.

   She advises they study Spanish soon.

5. Él propone que yo escriba un libro sobre esto.

   He proposes I write a book about this.

Exercises:

1. Translate these verbs that can be used to give suggestions or recommendations:

    a. To suggest

    b. To ask

    c. To ban

    d. To beg

    e. To recommend

    f. To advise

    g. To encourage

    h. To order

    i. To demand

    j. To insist

2. Mark the following sentences with a ✓ if they're written correctly and with a ✗ if they are wrong:

    a. Insisto en que cocinen comida italiana hoy.

    b. Pedimos que tengan mucha paciencia.

    c. Él escucha que sugiero camino rápido.

    d. Usted pide que abran la puerta.

    e. Nosotros rogar que hagan un plan.

    f. Ellas recomiendan que adopten un perro.

    g. Ruego que tú escribamos una carta.

    h. Vosotros sugerís que yo tomando una siesta.

    i. Tú dices que no salgamos de la casa.

    j. Ella insistir que nadar en el río.

3. Connect the sentences with the correct translation on the other column:

    a. Yo sugiero   1. We say

    b. Él ruega   2. I beg

    c. Usted pide   3. I suggest

    d. Nosotros decimos   4. You advise

    e. Ellas recomiendan   5. You ask

299

f. Tú insistes

g. Yo ruego

h. Él sugiere

i. Ella recomienda

j. Vosotros aconsejáis

6. He suggests

7. He begs

8. She recommends

9. They recommend

10. You insist

4. Complete these sentences with the translation of the verb in parenthesis:

   a. Nosotros (to suggest) _____ que cambies de coche.

   b. Ella (to recommend) _____ que bailemos juntos.

   c. Yo (to insist) _____ en que trabajen conmigo.

   d. Ángel (to say) _____ que escuchemos su argumento.

   e. Mi madre (to beg) _____ que no digamos mentiras.

   f. Tú (to ask) _____ que traiga regalos.

   g. Yo (to advise) _____ que compren este libro.

   h. Ellos (to propose) _____ que juguemos béisbol.

   i. Usted (to ban) _____ que caminen en el jardín.

   j. Vosotros (to suggest) _____ que hagamos ejercicio.

5. Write the subjunctive of the following verbs:

   a. Ella + pintar   _____

   b. Yo + escuchar   _____

   c. Tú + robar   _____

   d. Él + perder   _____

   e. Usted + salir   _____

   f. Tú + beber   _____

   g. Nosotros + tomar   _____

   h. Yo + pensar   _____

   i. Vosotros + mentir   _____

   j. Ella + decir   _____

<u>Translations:</u>

Translate the following sentences into English:

1. Pedimos a los pasajeros que permanezcan en sus asientos por ahora.

_____

2. Mi padre recomienda que yo aprenda a conducir este año.

_____

3. Yo aconsejo que no hagas clase a las siete de la mañana.

_____

4. Laura insiste en que pintemos nuestra casa de azul.

_____

5. Usted dice que escuchen la radio esta tarde.

_____

6. Él pide que visites la casa más a menudo.

_____

7. Recomiendo que escuches este grupo de música rock.

_____

8. Proponemos que trabajéis en equipos de tres personas.

_____

9. La policía aconseja que no pasemos por esta calle.

_____

10. Camilo sugiere que busques otro trabajo.

_____

Story:

A lo largo de la historia, la humanidad ha descubierto varias **verdades** universales. Estas son cosas que son ciertas, son **innegables**, y están científicamente comprobadas. Por ejemplo, todos sabemos que el sol saldrá cada mañana, que la tierra es **redonda**, y que la gravedad nos mantiene firmes en la **superficie** de la tierra. Pero hay algo más que a veces olvidamos, algo que todos hemos escuchado alguna vez en nuestras vidas y que, aunque lo dudemos, parece ser una verdad universal: Las madres siempre tienen la razón. Bueno, tal vez no siempre, pero sí parecen tener una habilidad especial para predecir ciertas cosas. Ahora, tan solo pido que imaginen cómo sería tener una verdadera **bruja** como madre.

Las brujas tienen mala reputación. Pero las brujas son mucho más que **sombreros**, **escobas**, y gatos negros. Esta es la historia de una bruja hermosa, inteligente, y con tres hijos que dudaban de sus poderes mágicos para ver el futuro. El primer hijo aprendió la lección fácilmente, cuando su madre dijo: "Sugiero que uses un jersey hoy; va a llover." El hijo no la escuchó, y al final del día estaba **mojado** por la lluvia. El segundo hijo **sufrió** un poco más, cuando su madre dijo: "Recomiendo que no te cases con esta mujer; es mala." El hijo no la escuchó, y su esposa le **robó** todo su dinero. El tercer hijo no quería saber el futuro, solo quería saber cuál era la verdad más grande en el universo. Su madre, la bruja, no dudo en responder: "La verdad más grande en el universo es mi amor por vosotros."

Vocabulary List:

1. verdades - truths
2. innegables - undeniable
3. redonda - round
4. superficie - surface
5. bruja - witch
6. sombreros - hats
7. escobas - brooms
8. mojado - wet
9. sufrió - suffered
10. robó - stole

Translated Story:

Throughout history, humanity has discovered several universal **truths**. These are things that are true, they're **undeniable**, and they're scientifically proven. For example, we all know the sun will rise every morning, the Earth is **round**, and gravity keeps us firmly on the **surface** of the Earth. But there is something else that we sometimes forget, something that we all have heard once in our lives, and that even if we doubt it, it seems to be a universal truth: Mothers are always right. Well, maybe not always, but they seem to have a special ability to predict certain things. Now, I just ask you to imagine how it would be to have a real **witch** as a mother.

Witches have a bad reputation. But witches are much more than **hats**, **brooms**, and black cats. This is the story of a beautiful, intelligent witch with three sons that doubted her magical powers to see the future. The first son learned the lesson easily, when his mother said, "I suggest you wear a sweater today; it's going to rain." The son didn't listen, and at the end of the day, he was **wet** by the rain. The second son **suffered** a little more, when his mother said, "I recommend you don't marry this woman; she's bad." The son didn't listen, and his wife **stole** all his money. The third son didn't want to know the future; he only wanted to know what the greatest truth in the universe was. His mother, the witch, didn't hesitate to answer, "The greatest truth in the universe is my love for you."

Questions:

1. ¿Cómo son las verdades universales? _____

   How are universal truths described?

2. ¿Cuál es la cuarta verdad universal mencionada? _____

   Which is the fourth universal truth mentioned?

3. ¿Para qué es la habilidad especial de las madres? _____

   What is the special ability of mothers for?

4. ¿Qué cosas caracterizan normalmente a las brujas? _____

   _____

   What things usually characterize witches?

5. ¿Cómo terminó el segundo hijo de la bruja? _____

   How did the second son of the witch end up?

6. ¿Quién robó el dinero del segundo hijo de la bruja? _____

   Who stole the money of the witch's second son?

Answers:

1.

        a. Sugerir

        b. Pedir

        c. Prohibir

        d. Rogar

        e. Recomendar

        f. Aconsejar

        g. Animar

        h. Ordenar

        i. Demandar

        j. Insistir

2.

        a. ✓

        b. ✓

        c. ✗

        d. ✓

        e. ✗

        f. ✓

        g. ✗

        h. ✗

        i. ✓

        j. ✗

3.

        a. a - 3

        b. b - 7

        c. c - 5

        d. d - 1

        e. e - 9

        f. f - 10

g. g - 2

h. h - 6

i. i - 8

j. j - 4

4.

a. sugerimos

b. recomienda

c. insisto

d. dice

e. ruega

f. pides

g. aconsejo

h. proponen

i. prohibe

j. sugerís

5.

a. pinte

b. escuche

c. robes

d. pierda

e. salga

f. bebas

g. tomemos

h. piense

i. mintáis

j. diga

Translations:

1. We ask the passengers to stay in their seats for now.

2. My dad recommends I learn how to drive this year.

3. I advise you don't take classes at seven in the morning.

4. Laura insists we paint our house blue.

5. You say to listen to the radio this afternoon.

6. He asks you to visit the house more often.

7. I recommend you listen to this group of rock music.

8. We propose you work in teams of three people.

9. The police advise we don't pass through this street.

10. Camilo suggests you look for another job.

Story:

1. Son ciertas, son innegables, y están científicamente comprobadas.

2. Las madres siempre tienen la razón.

3. Para predecir ciertas cosas.

4. Sombreros, escobas, y gatos negros.

5. Mojado por la lluvia.

6. Su esposa.

Chapter 24
PAST PERFECT

In this chapter, we are going to study a very subject. We are talking about the *Pretérito Pluscuamperfecto* in Spanish. This is known by other names like Antecopretérito, or Pluperfect, and it is the equivalent of the **Past Perfect** tense in English. So, if you know Past Perfect in English, this won't be so difficult. First, let's review a few things about this particular tense.

The Past Perfect, as well as the Pretérito Pluscuamperfecto, is a tense used to talk about actions or events that took place in the past *before* another action or event from the past. This means that the focus of the sentence will be an action that precedes another. This second action or event is a point of reference also from the past. Let's take a look at an example in English and its translation in Spanish:

Yo había comido cuando lavé los platos. - I had eaten when I washed the dishes.

There are a few important things to notice in this example that will explain everything you need to know about the Past Perfect:

- There are two actions in the sentence that take place in the past: eating (comer) and washing the dishes (lavar los platos).
- The first of these actions mentioned in the sentence took place before the second one: I ate and afterward I washed the dishes.
- Usually, the verb of the second action is written in the Past Simple form.
- The Past Perfect is the first half of the sentence, the first action.

The structure of the Past Perfect is as follows:

- **Subject** (this can be skipped in cases when it's redundant) **+ Verb *Haber*** (Imperfect form) **+ Past participle of the verb**
  - (Nosotros) Habíamos salido

The imperfect form of the Verb *Haber* (Have) is:

I had	Yo había
You had	Tú habías
He/She/It had	Él/Ella/Eso/Usted había
We had	Nosotros/as habíamos
You had	Vosotros/as habíais
They had	Ellos/as habían

To get the Past participle of a verb, the ending of the infinitive form of the verb changes from -ar to -ado, and from -er and -ir to -ido

- To speak: Hablar - Hablado
- To study: Estudiar - Estudiado
- To move: Mover - Movido
- To go: Ir – Ido

- There are also some irregular verbs like:
  - To say: Decir - Dicho
  - To writer: Escribir - Escrito
  - To do: Hacer - Hecho
  - To see: Ver - Visto

There are a few words that help identify Past Perfect sentences. They indicate that an action has or hasn't happened, or that it happened before another action. For example:

- Already: Ya
  - Yo ya había visto la película. - I had already watched the movie.

- When: Cuando
  - Tú habías ido a la fiesta cuando yo llamé. - You had gone to the party when I called.

- Before: Antes (que/de/de que)
  - Ella había bailado antes de que llegáramos. - She had danced before we arrived.

309

- Until: Hasta
  - Yo no había visitado a mi prima hasta ahora. - I hadn't visited my cousin until now.

- Yet: Todavía
  - Ellos no habían ido a la playa todavía. - They hadn't gone to the beach yet.

When writing negative sentences in the Past Perfect, "no" goes before the verb *Haber*.

- Nosotros no habíamos escuchado la alarma hasta ahora. - We hadn't heard the alarm until now.

When using reflexive pronouns (me, te, se, nos, se) in a Past perfect sentence, they are placed in front of the verb *Haber*.

- Tú **te** habías bañado cuando llegamos a visitarte. - You had taken a bath when we arrived to visit you.
- Ella no **se** había despertado cuando yo hice el desayuno. - She hadn't woken up when I made breakfast.
- Yo **me** había lavado las manos cuando vi la pintura. - I had washed my hands when I saw the paint.
- Nosotros **nos** habíamos conocido antes de vernos hoy. - We had met each other before seeing each other today.
- Ellos **se** llamaban Los Leones antes de llamarse Los Tigres. - They called themselves The Lions before calling themselves The Tigers.
- Usted no **se** había dormido cuando sonó la alarma. - You hadn't fallen asleep when the alarm sounded.

Examples:

1. Tú habías llegado a casa cuando llovió.
   You had arrived at the house when it rained.

310

2. Yo no había cambiado mi número de teléfono todavía.

   I hadn't changed my phone number yet.

3. Gabriela había cocinado la cena cuando llegué.

   Gabriela had cooked dinner when I arrived.

4. Ellos habían empezado a trabajar antes de que yo terminara.

   They had started to work before I finished.

5. Nosotros habíamos estudiado antes de ir a la fiesta.

   We had studied before going to the party.

Exercises:

1. Fill in the blanks with the appropriate conjugation of the verb *Haber*:

   a. Tú _____ conducido.

   b. Nosotros _____ viajado.

   c. Rosa _____ presentado.

   d. Yo no _____ comido.

   e. Él se _____ bañado.

   f. Vosotras _____ entrenado.

   g. Tú _____ trabajado.

   h. Ella _____ saltado.

   i. Rafael no _____ practicado.

   j. Nosotros nos _____ perdido.

2. Mark the following sentences with a ✓ if they're written correctly and with a ✕ if they are wrong:

   a. Tú habías renunciado cuando yo conseguí el trabajo. _____

   b. Nosotros nos habías bailado mucho cuando la canción terminó. _____

   c. Usted había cambiado de opinión cuando hablamos. _____

   d. Esteban se había casado cuando tú lo conociste. _____

   e. Ella bajado la escalera cuando ellos había abrir la puerta. _____

   f. Yo había estudiado inglés antes de aprender francés. _____

   g. Ellos habían tenis antes de jugar baloncesto. _____

   h. Vosotros habíais practicar antes de cantado juntos. _____

   i. Tú habías escrito cuentos antes de hacer libros. _____

   j. Elena había comprado un coche cuando le ofrecí el mío. _____

3. Write the Past Participle of the following verbs:

   a. Romper _____

   b. Dibujar _____

   c. Limpiar _____

   d. Correr _____

   e. Seguir _____

312

f. Besar   _____

g. Oler   _____

h. Actuar   _____

i. Herir   _____

j. Abrazar   _____

4. Fill in the blanks with the correct pronouns in the following sentences

   a. Tú habías bajado la escalera cuando (_____) subí.

   b. Él se había perdido cuando (_____) lo encontré.

   c. (_____) habíamos ganado cuando empezó la fiesta.

   d. (_____) habías salido cuando llovió.

   e. Yo había terminado los deberes cuando (_____) empezaste.

   f. Ella se había dormido cuando (_____) desperté.

   g. (_____) habías cerrado la puerta cuando ellos tocaron.

   h. (_____) me había bañado cuando el agua se fue.

   i. (_____) habíamos visto la película cuando fuimos al cine.

   j. Él había viajado a Colombia cuando (_____) pregunté por él.

5. Translate these Past Perfect sentences in English to Pretérito Pluscuamperfecto sentences in Spanish:

   a. We had met   _____

   b. You had crossed   _____

   c. I had danced   _____

   d. They had closed   _____

   e. We had fallen   _____

   f. She had written   _____

   g. I had built   _____

   h. You had planted   _____

   i. They had bought   _____

   j. He had dreamed   _____

Translations:

Translate the following sentences into English:

1. Antonio había encontrado la respuesta antes que yo lo hiciera.

_____

2. Tú habías llamado a la oficina antes de que ellos abrieran.

_____

3. Yo no había visto un lugar tan hermoso en toda mi vida.

_____

4. Ella había pintado la casa antes de mudarse.

_____

5. Vosotros habíais conocido a María antes de trabajar juntos.

_____

6. Los abuelos habían viajado a Europa antes de conocer África.

_____

7. Clara no había buscado un trabajo nuevo todavía.

_____

8. Yo ya había leído el libro cuando tú lo mencionaste.

_____

9. Usted había estado enfermo cuando lo invitamos a salir.

_____

10. Tú habías hecho los deberes cuando la biblioteca cerró.

_____

Story:

Pedro había sido un hombre muy **serio** toda su vida. Cuando era joven, había estudiado mucho antes de **convertirse** en abogado. Luego se casó con una mujer que amaba mucho, compraron una bonita casa, y tuvieron tres hijos. La vida de Pedro había cambiado completamente cuando sus hijos nacieron. Esos **delicados** bebés le inspiraban mucha **ternura** y un amor infinito. Sin embargo, los niños crecen. Pedro sentía que todo había cambiado de un día para otro. Sus hijos habían pasado de lindos bebés a ser niños **alegres**, y luego adolescentes complicados.

Pedro no había sospechado que tendría que usar su talento como abogado para tratar con sus hijos. Así descubrió que los niños son excelentes **mentirosos**, y que los hermanos se **apoyan** hasta el final. Cuando eran niños, Pedro les preguntó quién había roto la ventana. Cada uno de sus hijos **culpó** a otro, hasta que fue imposible descubrir al verdadero culpable. Cuando crecieron, Pedro les preguntó quién se había escapado de casa para ir a una fiesta. Cada uno de sus hijos **negó** haber escapado de casa, y Pedro no pudo **probar** que los tres habían ido a la fiesta juntos.

Vocabulary List:

1. serio – serious
2. convertirse - to become
3. delicados - delicate
4. ternura - endearment
5. alegres - joyful
6. mentirosos - liars
7. apoyan - support
8. culpó - blamed
9. negó - denied
10. probar - to prove

Translated Story:

Pedro had been a very **serious** man all his life. When he was young, he had studied a lot before **becoming** a lawyer. Then he married a woman he loved a lot; they bought a pretty house and had three children. Pedro's life had changed completely when his children were born. Those **delicate** babies inspired him with a lot of **endearment** and infinite love. However, kids grow up. Pedro felt that everything had changed overnight. His children had passed from pretty babies to being **joyful** kids and then complicated teenagers.

Pedro hadn't suspected he would have to use his talent as a lawyer to deal with his children. This way, he discovered that children are excellent **liars** and that siblings **support** each other until the end. When they were kids, Pedro asked them who had broken the window. Each one of his children **blamed** another one until it was impossible to discover who was the real culprit. When they grew up, Pedro asked them who had escaped from the house to go to a party. Each one of his children **denied** having escaped the house, and Pedro couldn't **prove** that the three of them had gone to the party together.

Questions:

1. ¿Cuál es el trabajo de Pedro? _____
   What is Pedro's job?

2. ¿Cuántos hijos tuvieron Pedro y su esposa? _____
   How many children did Pedro and his wife have?

3. ¿Cómo cambió todo? _____
   How did everything change?

4. ¿Quiénes son excelentes mentirosos? _____
   Who are excellent liars?

5. ¿Qué rompieron los hijos de Pedro? _____
   What did Pedro's children break?

6. ¿De dónde escaparon los hijos de Pedro? _____
   Where did Pedro's children escape from?

Answers:

1.

    a. habías

    b. habíamos

    c. había

    d. había

    e. había

    f. habíais

    g. habías

    h. había

    i. había

    j. habíamos

2.

    a. ✓

    b. ✗

    c. ✓

    d. ✓

    e. ✗

    f. ✓

    g. ✗

    h. ✗

    i. ✓

    j. ✓

3.

    a. Roto

    b. Dibujado

    c. Limpiado

    d. Corrido

    e. Seguido

    f. Besado

g. Olido

h. Actuado

i. Herido

j. Abrazado

4.

a. yo

b. yo

c. Nosotros

d. Tú

e. tú

f. me

g. Tú

h. Yo

i. Nosotros

j. yo

5.

a. Nosotros habíamos conocido

b. Tú habías cruzado

c. Yo había bailado

d. Ellos habían cerrado

e. Nosotros habíamos caído

f. Ella había escrito

g. Yo había construido

h. Tú habías plantado

i. Ellos habían comprado

j. Él había soñado

Translations:

1. Antonio had found the answer before I did it.

2. You had called the office before they opened.

3. I hadn't seen a place so beautiful in all my life.

4. She had painted the house before moving in.

5. You had met María before working together.

6. The grandparents had traveled to Europe before meeting in Africa.

7. Clara hadn't searched for a new job yet.

8. I had already read the book when you mentioned it.

9. You had been sick when we invited you to go out.

10. You had done the homework when the library closed.

Story:

1. Abogado.

2. Tuvieron tres hijos.

3. De un día para otro.

4. Los niños.

5. Rompieron la ventana.

6. Escaparon de la casa.

Chapter 25
VERBS WITH PREPOSITIONS

¡Felicidades! You've reached the final chapter of this guide for learning Spanish at an intermediate level.

At this point, you know more than just the basics of the Spanish language. You can do much more than craft a simple sentence and have a short conversation. These carefully and professionally crafted lessons have given you the tools to grow comfortable in this new language, be creative, experiment, and learn at your own pace and in your own style. These resources will be essential in the process of speaking Spanish naturally, correctly, and with the understanding of a native Speaker. Now, we have one more lesson to complete the process.

Right from the beginning, we've been familiar with the basic structure of a sentence in Spanish: the subject, the verb, and the complement (*sujeto, verbo, y complemento*).

In this chapter, we're going to pay special attention to the verbs, and we're going to dive deeper into the complexities of this part of the sentence. We're not talking about the different tenses of moods of a sentence that we've studied before. In this case, we will study the case of Verbs with Prepositions.

What exactly are we talking about? It's just as it sounds: the group of verbs that have a preposition to go along with them in a sentence.

What are prepositions? These are a series of words that serve to add context or additional information to a sentence, meaning that they will indicate how the object relates to the subject of the sentence. The most common pronouns in English are at, between, in, from, on, to, and with, but there are many, many more.

In English, we also use verbs that include a preposition to have the right meaning.

For example:

She believes **in** you.	I'm waiting **for** him.	We went **to** the party.

Notice how the sentence would change the literal meaning or even wouldn't make sense if we eliminated the prepositions:

She believes you.	I'm waiting him.	We went the party.

The same thing happens in Spanish. Let's take a look.

Ella confía **en** ti.	Yo espero **por** él.	Nosotros fuimos **a** la fiesta.
Ella confía ti.	Yo espero él.	Nosotros fuimos la fiesta.

Without the prepositions, the sentences wouldn't mean the same, or they would lose all meaning.

Here's a list of the most commonly used verbs with prepositions in Spanish, along with their translation in English and helpful examples to get you started on this subject.

	Verb with preposition	Meaning	Example
Preposition: "A"	Acostumbrarse a	to get used to	Yo me acostumbro a dormir temprano.
	Ayudar a	to help to	Tú me ayudaste a estudiar.
	Ir a	to go to	Él irá a la montaña.
	Jugar a	to play to	Ella jugó al tenis.
	Negarse a	to refuse to	Usted se negó a salir.
Preposition: "Con"	Casarse con	to marry with	Él se casó con ella.
	Colaborar con	to collaborate with	Nosotros

			colaboramos con ellos.
	Comparar con	to compare with	Tú te comparas con ella.
	Contar con	to count with	Yo cuento con vosotros.
	Soñar con	to dream of	Ella soñó conmigo.
Preposition: "De"	Acordarse de	to remember	Él se acordó de mi cumpleaños.
	Cuidar de	to take care of	Ella cuida de su madre.
	Enamorarse de	to fall in love with	Usted se enamoró de él.
	Hablar de	to talk about	Ellos hablaron de deportes.
	Tratar de	to try to	Nosotros tratamos de cocinar.
Preposition: "En"	Confiar en	to trust in	Tú confías en ellos.
	Creer en	to believe in	Usted cree en Dios.
	Insistir en	to insist in	Yo insistí en estudiar español.
	Participar en	to participate in	Ellos participarán en la carrera.
Preposition: "Por"	Disculparse por	to apologize for	Ellas se disculparon por el error.

	Esforzarse por	to try hard for (make an effort for)	Yo me esfuerzo por mejorar.
	Luchar por	to fight for	Tú luchas por tus derechos.
	Preguntar por	to ask for	Nosotros preguntamos por tí.
	Preocuparse por	to worry about	Él se preocupa por su problema.
	Interesarse por	To interested in	Ella no se interesa por la música

Note: Although some prepositions seem like they can be translated from English to Spanish, sometimes, verbs with prepositions will use a different kind of preposition in English and in Spanish.

Examples:

1. Yo no confío en este profesor.
   I don't trust this teacher.

2. Carlos se enamoró de mi hermana.
   Carlos fell in love with my sister.

3. Ella se disculpó por llegar tarde.
   She apologized for arriving late.

4. Tú te acostumbrarás a hablar español.
   You get used to speaking Spanish.

5. Ella no se quiere casar con él.
   She doesn't want to marry him.

Exercises:

1. Choose the right option to fill in the blank in each sentence:

   a. Nosotros _____ museo de ciencias.

      i. vamos al

      ii. comparar con

   b. Yo me _____ ella a primera vista.

      i. traté de

      ii. enamoré de

   c. Tú te _____ aprender a bailar.

      i. participas en

      ii. esfuerzas por

   d. Irene no se _____ el precio de la comida.

      i. preocupa por

      ii. contar con

   e. Mi padre se _____ mi madre hace veinte años.

      i. casó con

      ii. casarse con

   f. Mis hijos _____ policías y ladrones.

      i. cuidan de

      ii. jugaban a

   g. Vosotros _____ el presidente del país.

      i. olvidarse de

      ii. creéis en

   h. Ellos _____ comprar un coche.

      i. tardamos en

      ii. empezarán por

   i. Yo no _____ problemas del futuro.

      i. enamorar de

      ii. pienso en

   j. Ella _____ ver esa película.

      i. volvió a

      ii. ayuda a

2. Translate these verbs with prepositions from Spanish to their meaning in English:

325

a. Cambiar a   _____

b. Pensar en   _____

c. Hablar con   _____

d. Pasar por   _____

e. Olvidarse de   _____

f. Poner en   _____

g. Dirigirse a   _____

h. Conectar con   _____

i. Volver a   _____

j. Quejarse de   _____

3. Fill in the blanks with the correct preposition (a, con, de, en, por)

    a. Yo no participo _____ ninguna religión.

    b. Él se disculpó _____ su comportamiento.

    c. Karina amenazó _____ renunciar.

    d. Nosotros nos enfrentamos _____ un problema.

    e. Tú siempre contarás _____ tu familia.

    f. Usted tiene que tratar _____ descansar.

    g. Yo no dudo _____ pedir ayuda.

    h. El perro se acercó _____ la casa.

    i. Tú dejarás de ir _____ clases de inglés.

    j. Ellos se resistieron _____ venir.

4. Connect the verbs with prepositions in Spanish with their correct translation in English:

a. Luchar por	1. to be interested in
b. Empezar por	2. to settle for
c. Interesar por	3. to depend on
d. Convertir en	4. to fire
e. Depender de	5. to fight for
f. Cuidar de	6. to aspire to
g. Colaborar con	7. to collaborate with
h. Conformarse con	8. to begin with
i. Despedir a	9. to turn into

j. Aspirar a   10. to take care of

5. Write these sentences in the correct order:

    a. tú + la + a + profesora + ayudas

    _____

    b. estar + me + yo + alegro + de + aquí

    _____

    c. con + nosotros + ellos + colaboraremos

    _____

    d. su + familia + lucha + él + por

    _____

    e. se + niega + ella + a + trabajar

    _____

    f. usted + con + México + viajar + soñaba + a

    _____

    g. la + confían + en + ellos + ciencia

    _____

    h. me + animales + los + intereso + yo + por

    _____

    i. cuidaré + yo + ti + de

    _____

    j. novia + él + casar + se + con + su + quiere

    _____

Translations:

Translate the following sentences into English:

1. Los estudiantes no quieren colaborar con los profesores.

_____

2. Yo insisto en lavar el coche los días sábado.

_____

3. Mi hermano me ayudó a construir una casa en el árbol.

_____

4. Alejandro está hablando de la economía del país.

_____

5. El jefe preguntó por la secretaria nueva de la empresa.

_____

6. Yo le dije a mi madre que no se preocupe por mí.

_____

7. Tú tienes que participar en este proyecto grupal.

_____

8. Vosotros os negasteis a viajar en barco por el Mar Caribe.

_____

9. Lucía soñó con ir a un concierto de música jazz.

_____

10. Nosotros nos acordamos de cerrar la puerta en la noche.

_____

Story:

Desde que era una niña pequeña, Sara soñó con ganar el **concurso** de **disfraces** de Halloween. Cada año, en Halloween, en el colegio de Sara todos los estudiantes participaban en un concurso de disfraces. Era un gran evento. El ganador del concurso se llevaba una **bolsa** de dulces y la oportunidad de faltar a clase por una semana. Por ese motivo, todos se esforzaban por ganar. Sara se esforzaba más que todos los demás, pero año tras año alguien le ganaba. Cuando Sara se disfrazó de princesa, un niño construyó una **armadura** de caballero y ganó. Cuando Sara se disfrazó de pingüino, una niña se disfrazó de jirafa con un gran **cuello** y ganó. Incluso cuando Sara se disfrazó de vampiro, alguien se pintó todo el cuerpo de verde como Frankenstein y le ganó.

Eventualmente, Sara se graduó, fue a la universidad, hizo una familia, y empezó a trabajar. Veinte años después de su graduación, Sara fue **transferida** a esa misma escuela para trabajar como profesora. Pasaron un par de meses hasta que Sara se acordara del gran concurso de disfraces. Pero los profesores no participaban en él, así que no se esforzó mucho, tan solo se puso un vestido negro y una **peluca**. Sin embargo, cuando el concurso de disfraces estaba por **terminar**, la familia de Sara subió al **escenario**. Allí estaban su esposo, sus hijos, sus hermanos, y su madre. Ella era la única que faltaba para completar un disfraz grupal de la famosa Familia Adams. Una vez que Sara subió al escenario, le dieron el **premio** por el mejor disfraz de la historia del colegio.

Vocabulary List:

1. concurso - contest
2. disfraces - costumes
3. bolsa - bag
4. armadura - armor
5. cuello - neck
6. transferida - transferred
7. peluca - wig
8. terminar - finish
9. escenario - scene
10. premio - award

Translated Story:

Since she was a little girl, Sara dreamed of winning the **costume contest** on Halloween. Every year on Halloween, at Sara's school, all the students used to participate in a costume contest. It was a big event. The winner of the contest took a **bag** of candies and the opportunity to skip classes for a week. For this reason, everyone tried hard to win. Sara tried harder than everyone else, but year after year, someone beat her. When Sara dressed up as a princess, a boy built a knight's **armor** and won. When Sara dressed up as a penguin, a girl dressed up as a giraffe with a great **neck** and won. Even when Sara dressed up as a vampire, someone painted their entire body green like Frankenstein and won.

Eventually, Sara graduated, went to college, had a family, and started to work. Twenty years after her graduation, Sara was **transferred** to that same school to work as a teacher. A few months passed until Sara remembered the big costume contest. But the teachers didn't participate in it, so she didn't try very hard; she just put on a black dress and a **wig**. However, when the costume contest was about to **finish**, Sara's family went on the **stage**. There was her husband, her children, her brothers, and her mother. She was the only one missing to complete a group costume of the famous Adams Family. Once Sara went up on the stage, they gave her the **award** for the best costume in the history of the school.

Questions:

1. ¿Qué recibía el ganador del concurso? _____

    What did the winner of the contest receive?

2. ¿Quién se esforzaba más por ganar? _____

    Who tried hardest to win?

3. ¿Cuáles fueron los tres disfraces de Sara? _____

    What were Sara's three costumes?

4. ¿Cuánto tiempo ha pasado desde la graduación de Sara? _____

    How much time has passed since Sara's graduation?

5. ¿Qué se puso Sara para el concurso? _____

    What did Sara wear for the contest?

6. ¿Quiénes subieron al escenario? _____

    Who went up on stage?

Answers:

1.

    a. vamos al

    b. enamoré de

    c. esfuerzas por

    d. preocupa por

    e. casó con

    f. jugaban a

    g. creéis en

    h. empezarán por

    i. pienso en

    j. volvió a

2.

    a. to change to

    b. to think about

    c. to talk with

    d. to pass by

    e. to forget about

    f. to put in

    g. to direct oneself to

    h. to connect with

    i. to go back to

    j. to complain about

3.

    a. en

    b. por

    c. con

    d. a

    e. con

    f. de

g. en

h. a

i. a

j. a

4.

    a. a - 5

    b. b - 8

    c. c - 1

    d. d - 9

    e. e - 3

    f. f - 10

    g. g - 7

    h. h - 2

    i. i - 4

    j. j - 6

5.

    a. Tú ayudas a la profesora.

    b. Yo me alegro de estar aquí.

    c. Nosotros colaboraremos con ellos.

    d. Él lucha por su familia.

    e. Ella se niega a trabajar.

    f. Usted soñaba con viajar a México.

    g. Ellos confían en la ciencia.

    h. Yo me intereso por los animales.

    i. Yo cuidaré de ti.

    j. Él se quiere casar con su novia.

Translations:

1. The students don't want to collaborate with the teachers.
2. I insist on washing the car on Saturdays.
3. My brother helped me build a treehouse.
4. Alejandro is talking about the country's economy.
5. The boss asked about the new secretary of the company.
6. I told my mom not to worry about me.
7. You have to participate in this group project.
8. You refused to travel by boat across the Caribbean Sea.
9. Lucia dreamed of going to a concert of jazz music.
10. We remembered to close the door at night.

Story:

1. Una bolsa de dulces y la oportunidad de faltar a clases por una semana.
2. Sara.
3. Princesa, pingüino y vampire.
4. Veinte años.
5. Un vestido negro y una peluca.
6. La familia de Sara.

CONCLUSION

¿Cómo te sientes? How does it feel to complete another big step successfully? This isn't just a class or a series of lessons; this is part of your life. If you are reading this page, you have officially completed a whole new chapter of your life.

The knowledge you have acquired with the assistance of this book is something no one and nothing will ever take away from you. These lessons, these practical sentences, and priceless tips and recommendations will accompany you for the rest of your life. With this knowledge in Spanish, you'll be a whole new person, with a universe of opportunities opening up to you. There's no going back, but most importantly, this is far from the end.

A crucial quality of this guide is that it's so much more than a factual book. What you have finished reading is a tool. It is something that you can keep with you, reusing it as many times as necessary and in whichever way you feel best to do it. The success of this learning process is in your hands; you have made it this far, challenged, improved, and tested yourself. This is no small feat.

What comes next depends on your discipline, passion, and patience. We stand by the belief that anybody can learn a new language, and mastering the Spanish language is more than achievable if you really want it. With this book, this appropriate and useful guide, you have everything you need to make this dream a reality for you.

Within the 25 chapters of this book, we introduced new and exciting concepts that have elevated your basic knowledge of Spanish. Upon learning how to handle technical elements of the language, you have achieved a plethora of new possibilities to express yourself and understand others in this language.

These include the likes of the tricky reflexive and reciprocal verbs, the difference between indicative, imperative, and subjunctive moods, different adverbs, pronouns, and so much more. In Spanish, these technicalities are far from boring; they are fascinating challenges that will exercise important parts of your brain.

In no time, you will realize that even the subjects that seemed confusing and entirely unfamiliar start to come as easy as breathing when you use them in Spanish. The things that you have put a lot of effort into memorizing will never leave you. Every exercise and question we set you along the lessons served a specific purpose, and every time that you struggled, you came out of it with precious new knowledge. Through the translation tasks and the stories you experienced in English and Spanish, you've also exercised the skills you were collecting.

This was all done with the intent of making Spanish part of your life, perspective, and thoughts. Even if it might not seem like it at first, your brain is confidently starting to think in Spanish as a second language. All this training and dedication will pay off, and almost without noticing, every time you practice Spanish, it will come to you smoother and easier.

Eventually, you will personally see yourself experimenting and getting creative, being able to take bigger steps and explore new knowledge by yourself. That's the most wonderful part about your connection with this guide. You don't have to leave it behind now. These lessons are here for you to review, ask for guidance, open up again when you need to, and accompany you on the rest of the way toward fluency in Spanish.

The goal of this guide was to prepare the readers of this book for the rest of their journey, to provide them with the necessary information, and train them with specialized tests that will guarantee the absorption of the knowledge. With every page, you have come closer to becoming fluent in Spanish, and now, as you close this book, it's the real world that opens up to you as your next teacher. With endless opportunities to practice what you've studied so far, you will never stop learning.

It's been an honor to guide you on this journey. We can't wait to hear about the following fantastic things you'll achieve in your life with your brand-new Spanish skills.

¡Buena suerte!

Made in the USA
Middletown, DE
14 December 2022

18540104R00188